W9-BRI-067

The

Sweet Potato Queens'

Guide to Raising Children for Fun and Profit

JILL CONNER BROWNE

SIMON & SCHUSTER
New York   London   Toronto   Sydney

SIMON & SCHUSTER
1230 Avenue of the Americas
New York, NY 10020

For information about special discounts for bulk purchases,please contact Simon & Schuster Special Sales at 1-800-456-6798 or business@simonandschuster.com.

Designed by Dana Sloan

Manufactured in the United States of America

1   3   5   7   9   10   8   6   4   2

Library of Congress Cataloging-in-Publication Data
Browne, Jill Conner.
The Sweet Potato Queens' guide to raising children for fun and profit / by Jill Conner Browne.
p. cm.
1. Child rearing—Humor.   2. Motherhood—Humor.   I. Title.
PN6231.C315B76 2008
818'.5407—dc22   2007026786

ISBN-13: 978-0-7432-7836-2
ISBN-10:   0-7432-7836-4

To my only baby — Bailey — heart of my very heart
forever and always

≼ and ≽

To my second mama — Freda Katool Holmes — thanks for
my best friend, Cindy, and for the love and kisses
so freely given to ALL your kids

Contents

The Sweet Potato Queens' Guide to

Raising Children
for Fun and Profit

Hey, There!! Don't Skip This Part—It's Important!

For the uninitiated, the author of this book is a fairly renowned *humor* writer and she does purport for the most part only to make you *laugh*, preferably out loud, the sound accompanied by bodily emissions, both nasal and otherwise, but in the absence of those, will happily settle for the suppressed snicker and/or chortle. Occasionally, she will, either with intent or by complete accident, pass along the random bit of wisdom or otherwise useful snippet of information—these should be considered free bonuses to go along with the aforementioned chuckles.

This book is not intended to be a full statement or even a half-assed smattering of any actual scientifically tested methodology for the rearing of children—and yes, the author does know that children are reared, corn is raised—even the title is a joke, guys. Speaking of the title, specifically that *"Fun and Profit"* part—that is REEEALLY a joke. I mean, anybody who's ever had a kid or even known one knows that the experience is *neither* fun nor profitable.

The author just hopes this book provides even the briefest respite for the weary soul of the parent. Being a female-type mother herownself, the author does more specifically address here the plight of female-type mothers because that's the only area in which she has any experience at all. She is not now, nor has she ever been, a male-type father, and thus she can only judge them from her own perspective, and, admittedly, she generally finds them wanting. It is not, therefore, her intent to ignore or denigrate the role of fathers—so much as it is to ridicule same for the amusement of the mothers.

Parenting is the most incredibly full-time volunteer job ever—literally in the history of mothers—human and otherwise. Granted, *some* dads, human and otherwise, do help out—some help out a whole lot—but for the most part, in all species, if not for mothers, the whole thing woulda fallen apart aeons ago. God is nothing if not foresighted.

So, if you're a new mom who hasn't even hatched her first one yet—bless your heart—or if you're a seasoned veteran mom—bless your heart, too. God bless the hearts of any and all of us who help in any way, shape, or form to nurture the spirit, mind, and bodies of the children in this world. There are, after all, legions of true-in-every-sense-of-the-word *mothers* in our lives who did not give birth to us or to anybody else—and yet, without them, life for all would be immeasurably diminished.

Holy Shit!

The Cutest Boy in the World is a Man Who Can Fix Things. The man can fix anything—*anything*—even if he broke it first, he can fix it. He can build anything, unclog anything, hang anything, patch anything, retool, replumb, and/or rewire anything. (This is only one of his *many* gifts—but it's the one we're talking about at the moment. And the value of a man with the ability—and willingness—to fix things cannot be overstated.)

At times, even *he* is agog at his uncanny talent for fixing things—especially when it comes to electrical stuff. He says that as many times as he has performed the (for him) simple act of, say, installing a new light fixture and switch—he never ceases to be amazed when he flips the switch and the sumbitch actually *works*. This would be on account of Electricity is just a huge mystery of our universe. Yeah, yeah—there are countless electrical engineers and other geeks who can explain till those

3

proverbial bovines have their much-touted homecoming *how* it works, but *nobody* knows WHY. I mean, what a weird force of nature and how bizarre that we just take it for granted every minute of our lives—we just accept that if we plug it in, it works. I swear, you could make yourself crazy if you spent much time contemplating it—so don't—just every once in a while allow yourself a much-deserved moment of "holy shit" when the lights do, in fact, come on.

Well, in my opinion, getting pregnant is just like that. From the time you are a fairly small human, you have heard tell of *how* this is accomplished—and talk about *bizarre.* It is pretty earth-shattering news the first time you hear about it, no? But everybody pretty much knows what goes where and the potential outcome of it all, and on the surface it would seem to be pretty simple—I mean, even the dumbest *dog* on the planet has figured it out on his own, so how hard could it be?

Why it works is the big fucking (excuse the pun) mystery. Conception is easy to explain, but *copulation* is mind-boggling, even to people who've been doing it for more than fifty years— it is just such a weird thing to do with another person if you really stop to think about it. (Probably best if you don't, though—could be off-putting. And it seems to me that the Creator of the Universe *could* have made the whole thing a bit more dignified—but, then again, He could prolly tell right off that we were destined to take ourselves *way* too seriously and, boy hidee, is *this* ever a surefire remedy.)

When you first hear the news—either in the corner of a school yard from a smug classmate who really *does have* the SCOOP of the century or from a squirming parent who would rather be set on fire than have this Discussion—no matter where the info comes from, on one level you are completely floored, terrified, embarrassed, and confused, and on another level some part of your humanness just accepts it as fact.

More likely than not, no matter where your info comes from, the focus of it will be on CON-CEPTION and, more important, the fact that most of the rest of your life will be devoted to the CONTRA of it all—what all can and should be done to avoid conceiving—and we'll discuss the *volumes* of *mis*information about *that* later.

But when somebody tells you about sex for the first time, they're not *ever* telling you with the thought in mind of helping you figure out how to *get* pregnant—correctly surmising that, even though you're only ten, even you have got sense enough to know that you prolly oughta hold off on starting a family.

Nothing exists in the universe that can actually *prepare* you for that incredible moment in time when your very own eyes see that your very own personal urine has changed the color on that dipstick. You have been peeing since time began for you— never giving it much thought at all except in unusual circumstances that could involve anything from dialysis to Porta Potties, or the lack thereof—and now, all of a sudden, that regular pale warm stream that flows from your nether regions has delivered what is no less than the absolute *Death Knell* to what *used to be* your LIFE.

It matters not whether you are forty-five and have been hoping with nothing short of desperation to conceive or sixteen and utilizing nothing but desperate hope as your means of contraception—that *moment* when you know with absolute certainty that you are, in fact, a Pregnant Woman—I'd have to say it's the single Most Stunning Moment of Your Life. You've heard about it for years—and you've been following the steps like every other creature on the planet and nothing has ever happened—you've flipped that light switch to no avail for so long you've become accustomed to the dark, and now, all of a sudden, the same little flip of the same little switch has made some kind of cosmic connection and WHOOOO-DOGGIES, EVERY LIGHT IN THE HOUSE CAME ON!

HO-LY SHIT and then some! From this moment on *nothing* in your life will *ever*—EVER—EVER!—be the *same.*

Who knew it would ever really work? I mean, I still don't actually *believe* that airplanes can *fly*—I just suspend disbelief every time I get on one and somehow I magically end up in another place when I get off. It came as a complete and utter shock to me that *my* having sex would ever result in an actual *baby,* growing, even more shockingly, in *me.*

I was thirty-five when it happened to me for the first and only time. Now, suffice it to say that during my thirty-five trips around the sun I had also simultaneously made quite a few trips around The Block, so to speak, and not one of those trips had produced anything tangible. Truth be told, a whole big lot of 'em didn't produce much in the way of IN-tangibles *either*, but substandard sex, while disappointing, is not generally found to be life changing.

And then all of a sudden . . . I can't think of anything that sounds big enough to put here. It's like one of those *other* consequences your mother has threatened you with your entire life—"Don't do that, you're gonna put your eye out" kinda thing. Parenthetically speaking, I had long wondered why the absolute Worst Case Scenario is Mother's only one. You never get a "Don't do that, you might get a bruise"—no, it's always certain mutilation.

But we discovered that, quite often, really, Mama was Wrong. Out of her sight and supervision, we may not have exactly pushed the envelope, but we at least went up to the sticky part—and none of the bad things Mama had warned about happened to us. We double-headed on our sister's bike and our toes did not get cut off in the spokes. We crossed the street from between parked cars and our heads were not smashed like pumpkins beneath the tires of the oncoming vehicles. We went into the deep end and did not drown—even though our danger of same was compounded by the fact that it had been somewhat less than thirty minutes since we had eaten. We spoke to a stranger and he did not snatch us. We went to bed with our hair wet and we did not wake up with pneumonia.

How could this be? It seemed to us that Mama was just a big chicken who was afraid of absolutely everything and apparently did not know shit-diddly about anything.

Threats regarding anything to do with the opposite sex were no less foreboding. Our mamas didn't actually *say* it, but they certainly left us with the distinct impression that virtually *any* contact with a boy would lead immediately and forthwith to pregnancy—not to mention insurmountable shame and utter degradation. That anybody *ever* had sex after such admonitions is purely a testament to just how reeeeally swell sex is.

A young Queen from Starkville, Mississippi, had her jets significantly cooled for a goodly spell by her mother's assurance that should a boy fondle the breasts of the young woman, *milk* would squirt out. Mothers, bless their hearts . . . best intentions in the world.

Eventually, most of us would come to test Mama's accuracy in this and other areas as well. We would find a boy we thought irresistible and kiss him till our collective lips nearly peeled off our faces. And 99 percent of us waited to see if we would, in fact, become pregnant. Such was the state of mis/disinformation we got from our mamas—it was not unusual for a twelve- or thirteen-year-old girl to be worried a *year* after the kissing that she might one day just "turn up" pregnant.

People in the South are always—to this very day—"turning up" pregnant. Well, I say "people"—it's really only ever women, even down here. But that term has served to confuse and alarm many a Southern teenager, I can attest. There was never any kind of time line attached to this turning up so as far as we knew—the pregnancy could present itself at any time, without warning, and months, even years, after the childish act of supposed indiscretion.

But, as we *now* know, nobody ever turns up pregnant from kissing, and as that fact made itself known to us, we ventured out a bit farther on the, ahhh, limb and found it sturdy enough as well. For instance, French kissing. I had no idea what this was when, as a geeked-out seventh-grader, I first heard it mentioned in the girls' locker room at Peeples Junior High in Jackson, Mississippi. Confused and consumed with curiosity, I came dutifully home and asked my mother whatever could this French kissing thing *be*. And Mama looked very grave as she told me that it was "an invitation to a Lower Level." That was the sum total of the explanation I got for "French kissing." I went away and pondered on it for a while. My later attempts to extract from her any elaboration on the subject (for instance— by "lower level," what did she mean? Lower on one's person? Or did it refer to one's social status that would no doubt be lowered if one accepted such an invitation—see above re: pregnancy, shame, and degradation) yielded nothing. Apparently, that was all Mama knew or was willing to reveal about the subject because she held firm to her one line: It's an invitation to a Lower Level—and that's all you need to know about it.

Hmmmm . . . but I thought I needed to know a whole *lot*

more about it. I thought I might just need to know all there *was* to know about it, and I was pret-ty danged sure there *was* more to know about it than Mama was lettin' on.

And as it turned out, there were a whole bunch of folks in my circle who were every bit as confused and curious about this French kissing thing as I was. Luckily, there were at least a *few* who were not quite as confused as the rest of us—they led the way and pretty soon we were all going to parties at Gail's house. I'm not sure Gail had parents—you couldn't prove it by any of *us*—she appeared to be a cute adolescent girl, normal in every way except that she owned her own home—and thus, she was able to host these incredible make-out parties and we *lived* for them.

If you're entertaining on a budget, I can offer this as a very inexpensive and *very* festive party idea. There were absolutely no refreshments served—so that's a huge savings right there. Only two songs were played on the stereo all night—"House of the Rising Sun" and "Ebb Tide"— so no big outlay for tunes. The lights were off the whole time—so no need for decorations not to mention zero strain on your utility bill. "Seating" was not an issue since couples were simply splayed out on, around, and under any and all surfaces, regardless of whether or not they were actual pieces of furniture intended to be occupied by human bodies.

Upon entering through the darkened kitchen, everybody somehow paired off with a member of the opposing sex and immediately fell to making out—on chairs, sofas, countertops, on the piano and under it. The only action was mouth-to-mouth, but I can tell you, it was as entertaining an evening as I have ever spent in my en-tire life. (I blissfully shared spit and space under the Steinway with the dark-eyed heartthrob Conner Smith.) And I'm quite certain that all attendees would concur with this summation.

Although, come to think of it, it is prolly more appealing to the seventh- and eighth-grade set than, say, anybody three or more years out of puberty—but you know your crowd better than I do, so you might toss out the idea and see what they think. I will tell you that at our thirty-fifth class reunion, those of us who lived long enough to attend were STILL talking about Gail's parties—so I'm just sayin' . . .

And *that's* how I came to know for a *fact* that French kissing will definitely *not* cause you to turn up pregnant.

Still had some untested areas, though. There was much talk—MUCH talk—about these assorted "bases" and who all had "been to" which ones. More confusion and WAY more curiosity—and even *less* info forthcoming from Mom. She had never heard of any "bases," there was simply no such thing— that was just "kids talking." Hmmmm.

Well, they were definitely doing *that* and plenty of it—but it wasn't eggzackly a *documentary*-type discussion that was going on, and it appeared to me that nobody was really that much better informed than I was—except that they had at least somehow *heard* about the "bases" from some source that was currently unavailable to me.

I did have this older seester—Judy—but there was six years' difference in our ages, so at the time that I was *reeeally* needing this info, she was already off at college—*practicing* up, night and day, with all the info *she* knew, and our relationship was not yet at the stage where we would openly discuss the most intimate, minute details of Life as we knew it. So I was clueless and without hope.

Luckily, everybody else was pretty much in the same boat—although we were all totally *pretending* to one another that *we knew stuff*. It was as if we had picked up a foreign dictionary and memorized a few words phonetically—but the definitions were also in the foreign language, so all we had was the words themselves sans meaning. Kinda like thinking you're saying "Which way is the restroom?" in Spanish but what you actually said was, "Go away, I do not speak Chiclets."

But, then, the *worst* was when some of our older seesters actually did tell us some words and what they meant—for instance, *boobs* and *twat*. But *we* thought that our clever older seesters had *made up these words theirownselves* in order to talk *in code* in front of Stupid Grown-ups. And so we went around saying them all the time—even formed a *club*—we were the Twat Sisters—and oh, how funny, funny, funny we thought *that* was because *nobody in the world but us* (and our big seesters) *knew what a twat was*, and how clever were *we*?

And we made up little membership cards with *our names on them* and everything and were just prancing around junior high school—in the very early sixties—talking freely and loudly about our "boobs" and "twats" and our little club—thinking WHAT a great joke—because NOBODY KNEW WHAT IT MEANT BUT US (and our big seesters). And, as it turned out, the principal.

Mr. Measells overheard talk of a "secret club," and at that time in Mississippi, all secret societies, sororities, and fraternities were forbidden to children in public schools, and the school officials took the enforcement of this edict *very* seriously. Luckily, the one who got caught with her Twat Sisters Membership Card was Not Me. It was my friend Debbie—who was Miss Everything, all-American, girl-next-door, biggest-sweetest-smile-in-the-world cheerleader and well-known Good Girl, and so, of course, he totally believed her that there really was no "club," it was just a joke based on these few silly secret words that our big seesters had made up and shared with us.

Somehow he managed to keep a straight face as he advised her that they were *not secret words at all* and that pretty much everybody in the *world* knew *eggzackly* what they meant. And I imagine that it took a second or so for *that* happy news to sink in.

I am grateful to God to *this very day* that it was Not Me that had to have that conversation with Mr. Measells—whom I towered over, even in the seventh grade. I loved Debbie to bits and would not have wished for her anything but the absolute very best life has to offer—but man, was I ever glad she was the one who got caught. For one thing, one or two of the other Twat Sisters did not have quite the sterling sparkle to their reputations that Deb had (some even had pierced ears—although Mama didn't know it and that's the only reason I was allowed to hang out with 'em—"Only Whores Have Pierced Ears" was yet another Mama-ism), and had Mr. Measells not been so totally willing to accept as truth Debbie's account of the Twat Sisters Club and its origins, we might have all been suspended—yet another offense that toted a tag of "insurmountable shame and utter degradation" in those days.

I mean . . . something like that would *definitely* go in your Permanent Record. In the 1950s South, we were informed in the first grade that a file bearing our name had been opened (our Permanent Record), that the information about our comportment would be duly recorded in said file, and that it would follow us *all the days of our life*. Once something was installed in your Permanent Record—That Was It—you could never get it out no matter what. We obviously lived in mortal dread of committing any transgression that could somehow wind up inscribed in our Permanent Record. No telling how many actual felonies were prevented by this threat.

If you had a black mark in your Permanent Record, even if it was for something you did in the fifth grade, you could forget joining Chi O when you got to Ole Miss eight years later, and if you thought the Junior League would turn a blind eye to such obvious criminal traits, you got several more thinks coming.

You would never be able to get a decent job—because your Permanent Record would be the *first* thing any prospective employer would look at. And you could never get your hands on your Permanent Record—it was a top-secret set of documents held by the school system, and they would release it only to other people who wanted to know what it said about you before they hired you or let you join their organization or gave you a loan—you could never see the damning words in your Permanent Record, you could only suffer their effects.

Apparently, this, too, was a sham our mothers made up in their desperate attempts to civilize and control us. On account of I can name you at least 183 people—male and female and everything in between—who were, by anybody's definition, genuine *thugs* with Permanent Records a foot thick when we were growing up, and they, every one of 'em, not only lived to adulthood without losing any important body parts but went on to have mostly productive lives, and some of 'em were even able to join the Junior League (except the ones from South Jackson, of course—some things simply can*not* be overcome).

But, I digress—big surprise.

It was the pure and spotless Debbie who got caught and her capture brought about the end of the Twat Sisters and there were no indelible black marks in anybody's Permanent Records regarding membership in that organization. And don't you just know *that* woulda turned the Junior League on its ear if they'da come across *that* little notation about a prospective member? Might as well have a tattoo.

When the mama of one of my former Queens first caught her first glimpse of the very large tattoo festooning the back of the young and wayward Queen, her response was a gasping, "Well! You'll never get in the Junior League with *THAT!*"

Every little girl grows up around gatherings of women — which means by the time she reaches puberty, she's heard so many Labor and Delivery Nightmare stories, she's numb to them and any power they might have to dampen her burgeoning libido. Although at least a few of us did seem to make it to teenage in blissful ignorance of these tales. Okay, there was only one. Queen Tammy (her real name) was in her late teens before she was disabused of the notion that belly buttons just sort of iris'd open like old camera lenses and the baby just popped out, all pretty and pink, like a doll. I have never heard anything like this from anybody else on the planet before or since. I can only imagine Tammy's complete outrage when she learned the truth. But since she's the only one in the world who ever believed this yarn (and was it a yarn told to her or did she make it up herownself in the absence of any other data? I'm not sure), I don't think we have to be too concerned with making sure it gets refuted.

No, most everybody else got the scare tactics and, for anybody interested in attempting to dissuade a young girl from engaging in sexual activity prematurely, I would like to suggest—in place of the tales of Four Days and Nights of Hard Labor, Surly Cruel Delivery Room Nurses, and Failed Epidurals—try planting these seeds of horror in her mind's eye: big giant nipples and episiotomies. Oh, yeah. You want to make Abstinence more appealing—clue 'em in on these nuggets of knowledge.

Had anybody *ever hinted* to me that—with my olive complexion—during pregnancy my own personal nipples would grow to the size of salad plates and turn *black*—I can assure you, it would have given me Pause.

Most of our mamas spent all their time dispensing prophecies of degradation and ruin, and factual information about sex—specifically contraception—was never discussed. This was—and still is for many—considered to be Permission if not out-and-out *encouragement* to have unmarried teenage sex. It has been my observation—and experience—that hardly anybody needs encouragement to have sex. The hormones just sorta take over that job, unbidden.

And people—of any age—are *going* to *have* sex when *they* decide to—whether they have any information or not—and there won't be any parents around when they make that decision, so it's too late to be handing out facts then.

I know a sweet young thing who started having sex with her now-husband when she was just a young teen. Being the daughter of a policeman who apparently subscribed to the information-is-permission school of thought, she and her boy-lover relied solely on a contraception method that is as old as sex itself—and was proven to be ineffective about nine months after the first time it was ever tried on earth by humans, and what did they name that kid? Was it Cain or Abel? That would be the ole jerk-and-squirt, or, if you're Baptist, the pull-and-pray. They thought themselves quite the self-taught sexual sophisticates—until, of course, she "turned up" pregnant.

Sweetie learned about all the different kinds of contraception *after* her baby was born and she was married at sixteen to that young man who is now a preacher. And ten years later, she and her preacher man are remembering their own youthful indiscretions and asking themselves the burning question— Wonder who rebels the most in life—cops' kids (Mama) or preachers' kids?—as they watch their daughter head inexorably toward Teenage. They're praying for the former, of course!

But whether you're a scared, uninformed teenager or a scared, fairly well-educated thirty-five-year-old, the common denominators are there: shock, disbelief, and not a little fear.

At any rate, when you first learn that you are, in fact, *pregnant* and you have the experience of 1+ 1 equaling 3 (or more!), it is simply astounding because something your mama threatened you with *finally* came true, and from that moment on, your mama is about to get just a *whole* lot *smarter.*

Try to Appreciate the Weirdness

Okay, so you get irrefutable proof that you *are* pregnant—it takes a little while for that to *really* sink in and this is a pleasant and magical time—moment, really—in your pregnancy. Then your body starts to change. Now, if our mamas really wanted to scare us into abstinence, this is the info that they ought to have been putting out there.

I had that "pink cloud" of magical thinking about My Pregnancy for about a nanosecond before I began to detect the changes in my body. Somewhere around seventy-two hours after conception, I think, I gained about twelve pounds—all of it on my *back*. Nobody mentioned this likelihood when they were trying to dampen my budding libido. See, when you're pregnant, your back goes, like, *away* somehow. The front of your body gets impossibly long and your back gets short and fat. This same look is replicated in beer-bellied men, by the way.

Okay, let me pause right here and say that I am writing this book for *normal* people who, during pregnancy, blow up like Fat Elvis, eat everything that doesn't run off, cry at cotton commercials, and make unreasonable demands on their spouses coupled with tearful threats to run away if these demands are not met. By the beginning of the second trimester, they have outgrown everything they own but one pair of blue sweatpants and a size 10X sweatshirt, but they don't care, that's all they feel like wearing anyway, and then they give birth to something smaller than a grocery-store chicken. If this sounds like you, you are my people.

I have nothing to say to women who gained three pounds overall, ran marathons in tiny, strikingly coordinated outfits all the way to the delivery room, and weighed ten pounds less when they went home from the hospital than they did before they even got pregnant. Well, there are a couple of words I could muster, but they have just been done to death—I have nothing original to add. We might turn out to be kindred spirits, but we're gonna have a rocky start. There might be hope for you when we get to the part where they send you home with that baby—that can be a great equalizer. Big difference between childbearing and child rearing, as we will see.

Before I got pregnant, my weight had been absolutely stable for years on end. Couldn't gain a pound on a bet. Ate like a field hand, gobbled like a hawg—night and day—and beer, I drank a lot of beer, too—and I never, ever missed dessert (often eating entire pies at one sitting—really)—and the scales never betrayed me by so much as an ounce. This ability—to drink and eat with fervor and delight with no corresponding weight gain—does foster in one a certain smugness and a lack of empathy for others who have not received such metabolic blessings, and this is not something that is taken lightly by Karma.

And so it came to pass that not only did my entire body seem to be inflating before my eyes—but the scale would reveal wild fluctuations on an almost hourly basis. I might weigh myself first thing in the morning and be only mildly horrified at the poundage—only to pass the scale casually around noon and step on to discover I'd gained *six pounds* in four hours. Then, after exercising, I might weigh again and see that I'd lost five, but by bedtime there would be an additional several.

Suddenly, I was obsessed with the scale. I was weighing myself twenty-five to thirty times a day—I couldn't stop myself—and it was never good news. And so I made an Executive Decision (as a pregnant woman, you are *The* Chief Executive of your entire world—literally, *whatever* you say goes)—I decided that I would spend my entire pregnancy blissfully unaware of what the scale was saying about me—and it was gonna have to say it behind my back if it was gonna say it at all. Because that's how I got on the scale at Dr. Rascal Odom's office every month—backward.

I would lumber in and hold on to his precious nurse Connie's hand and step up with my back to the numbers, talking loudly to Connie all the while so that I couldn't hear the sound of her ooching the weights farther and farther across the bar as I packed on the pounds.

Not only did I refuse to look at it, I refused to listen to it—no one was allowed to *tell* me what I weighed nor to admonish me in any way about it. Dr. Rascal, of course, expressed some degree of dissatisfaction with this setup initially, but I told him that I was not gonna come outta this deal with an eating disorder—that I was sick of freaking out over the scale all day every day. I pointed out to him that I was over six feet tall, healthy, and slightly underweight when all this started, and if I had to pick somebody to be unhappy about my weight for the next nine months, I'd pick *him*, hands down.

If there were any other pregnant patients in the weigh-in area when I arrived, Connie would make every effort to herd them into another area—mutiny was inevitable if my secret was revealed. I gained and I gained and I gained—but at least I got to do it in peace. That peace was ultimately shattered, of course, when they sent me home from the hospital with a little baby girl who accounted for only a bit more than seven of the sixty-four pounds I'd put on during the manufacturing process.

I had seen hundreds—thousands—of pregnant women in my lifetime and heard countless tales of countless pounds packed on—never to be lost again in this life. Never did I imagine it happening to ME. This would seem to be an important point missing from the Abstinence materials I've seen.

I did not personally experience morning sickness—not ever, not one time. This, I believe, is because I staunchly refused to throw up and I advised the baby inside me in no uncertain terms that although we were currently sharing space formerly occupied by only me myownself, she was welcome to stay as long as she followed the house rules. I was not in the habit of starting each day with vomiting, and I had no intention of taking up the practice now—if there were any sudden bouts of nausea around here, I'd know whom to blame for it.

Popsicles and chicken-fried steak were the objects of my intense cravings. The Popsicles were a new development and, for the first time since grade school, I ate 'em by the boxful. The chicken-fried thing was more of an enhancement of a previously existing condition. There is a restaurant in downtown Jackson called the Elite (pronounced by most Jacksonians, myself included, as the E-light) that serves THE best chicken-fried steak on the planet, and everybody in Austin, Texas, needs to just haul ass over here and *try* it for theirownselves and then go back home and fill up on water, 'cause they ain't *got* no chicken-fried steak over there that even comes close.

It is possible to order "double meat" at the Elite—which is what I did about every other night during my en-tire pregnancy. I would order it with a big grin and tell the precious waitress that, after all, I *was* eating for two—and *one* of us—the one doing both the orderin' and the eatin'—was *great big* and mighty hongry. It's really a wonder I gained only sixty-four pounds.

Oh, there was one other thing I ate a whole lot of and that was Frusen Glädjé ice cream, which I don't think you can even get anymore prolly on account of I ate it all up in 1987. It had about 95 percent butterfat or something like that and, man alive, was it ever good. The "reason" I was eating so much of it, though, was because it came in the cutest little plastic containers that I knew would be just so handy to have around for leftovers and such—after the baby came. In retrospect, I suppose

Tupperware would have been significantly cheaper and literally calorie-free. Not as tasty, though.

So that's another weird thing that happens to you when you're pregnant—you lose your mind. I ate approximately 2 million calories' worth of ice cream—for the little buckets it came in—as if that made perfect sense—and Queen Cheryl had huge memory lapses. Two of the more significant occurrences were once when she couldn't remember how to start the car—which continues to be an important thing for her to know every single day of her life—and the other when she went to introduce her husband to somebody and she couldn't remember his NAME—which, in later years, became of no importance whatsoever.

Queen Ramona turned bad—sooo bad. When she was *real* pregnant, around eight and a half months or so of Real, her husband decided they needed more life insurance. So the insurance guy came out to the house to get all the paperwork done and he asked the husband all the questions about his health and family history and whatnot, and he wrote it all down and then started with the same questions for Ramona. He asked her if she'd ever been turned down (this is where she went bad)—she started batting her eyelashes at the guy and rubbing her big ole belly and she said, just as Southern as she could drawl out, "Why-y-y-y, no-o-o-o-o!" She let it hang there for a second, and then she looked all surprised and said, "Oh! You mean for *in*-surance?"

Every little pregnancy bonus that Mother Nature gives us comes with its own corresponding slap in the face with a wet squirrel. For instance, those of us who, in Normal Life, couldn't cleave on a bet suddenly find that in Pregnant World, we have tits for days—big, voluptuous, cleaving breasts overfill our every bra. But most everything south of them grows exponentially at the same time, which is not nearly as entertaining for us, or for the spectators.

I heard just the other day from a sweet little young thing whose mother-in-law had advised her to replace her bikini underwear with something more substantial when she bought maternity clothes. Oh, little young sweetie was horrified at the thought, and she was quite certain that since her undies didn't come up to the area that was going to be swelling soon, they would fit just fine for the duration of her pregnancy. She thought mom-in-law was a silly dinosaur with no knowledge of modern panties. Figuring that this prehistoric woman is prolly about my age, I silently took her side and said nothing. I just hope the mother-in-law has the satisfaction of being at Wal-Mart with little missy the day her bikini falls down around her ankles. Pantie styles may indeed evolve over time, but pregnant bellies haven't changed much since panties were invented, or since pregnancy was invented, for that matter—and what stayed up just fine prepregnancy is destined to be a boot-topper for those who choose to resist The Inevitable: Big Ones.

And, if you're still holding out, let me just tell you that once you experience the joy of a big, giant pair of cotton bloomers, you will never want little tiny panties again in this life. Yes, it's true. You will be Somebody's Mother and you will no longer give a rat's ass if your panties cover your belly button—and you will care even less if they match your bra! I can hear your horrified gasping. I'm sorry to just blurt it out like that—but somebody had to tell you. It's over. "Lingerie" is a sweet memory from your past—that will seem more distant with every passing year of breast-feeding, diaper changing, carpooling, and room mothering.

You will never go into Victoria's Secret again—unless, of course, you get a divorce—but that's all covered in my other book. In this book, we're hoping that your baby-daddy will be around for the duration—so with that hope firmly held, it's time to shop for grannypanties and get happy with 'em.

Another dual surprise—half happy, half not really *un*-happy, but really surprising and bizarre—is your hair. The hair on your head is all of a sudden perfect. You will have more hair than you've ever had in your life and it will be fabulous. But, true to her contrary form, Mother Nature has another gift for you. At the very same time that you are reveling in your new coiffure, a good ways down from your head, you will also find you suddenly have more hair than you've ever had in your life, and I don't know that I would say it's fabulous, necessarily. Not *un*-fabulous, I guess, but it's just so . . . unexpected. After puberty has run her course, one doesn't really anticipate any more changes—"down there"—and so when all of a sudden it appears that the little kitty is turning into a she-bear, well, it's just a surprise is all.

Of course, I vaguely knew about C-sections, but at no time had anybody ever made any reference, obscure or otherwise, to the possibility of any *other* sort of incision-type business associated with childbirth. Where were the people with *this* info? I never heard squat about it until I found myself in childbirth classes. *Fine* time to be hearing about *this*, I'm thinking. There were six youngish women, all sitting or lying on the floor with our pillows and our husbands, ignorant faces bright with anticipation, eager to learn about the last installment of our pregnancies, and all of a sudden the teacher/nurse starts talking about cutting us from stem to stern, as it were—in order to *try* to avoid *tearing*. Tearing, you say? Whoa nelly, just hold the phone now, Herman—tearing *what*? Ain't nobody never said nothin' 'bout no TEARIN'—we ain't studyin' on nothin' bein' *tore*. Oh, and then the video started. Now, that right there is some surefire birth control, if you ask me. I can name you six women right off the top of my head—from that very class—that woulda backed out of the deal right then and there if they could have.

I was pret-ty sure after that class that I was gonna be needin' me a nice, predictable, well-thought-out *Caesarean.* My friend Queen Vickie was actually able to finagle herself one by devious means—but she did it only because she was hungry.

When she and David married, she'd already had two kids from her previous marriage to "the ugly little man." (There is apparently photographic support for this nomenclature.) It was several years before she and David were able to get pregnant (although, as she pointed out and we already know—it was really only *she* that got pregnant)—so she was known to her doctor as "one of his old mothers," and she assumed that, as such, she would qualify automatically for a C-section.

It was a particularly hot day in August when she woke up feeling like it might be a good day to have a baby, and when she called the doctor, he told her, yep, sounded like it was time, come on in. Thinking she was headed for surgery—and would therefore be denied *lunch*—she popped into the 7-Eleven on her way to the hospital to grab a quick Dr Pepper and some peanuts—just to tide her over till suppertime.

Apparently, this behavior was not unusual. For some women, the onset of labor pains creates not only a mighty appetite but also a fear of famine, and all they can think about is getting a little something on the way to the hospital. My own personal seester, Judy, who gave birth to the wonderboy Trevor in the city of New Orleans, hopped off the streetcar and grabbed a cheeseburger on her way to the delivery room.

(I did, happily for me, end up requiring a section, and it was all planned out ahead of time so I never went into labor and did not experience the accompanying hunger pangs. I was, however, vitally concerned with the potential pangs of Others.

Before dawn on the appointed day, I was up making ten thousand or so ho-made blueberry muffins—not for myself, but for every shift of nurses that I might encounter for the next twenty-four hours—in hopes of bribing my way into the hearts of any Ratchet-type nurses that might be on duty. I've always felt it was time well spent.)

Anyway, fortified with her peanuts and Dr Pepper, Vic made her way to the hospital, where she was met by her husband, David. David and the doctor decided it was prolly going to be a long haul and they prolly oughta fortify themselves with a bite to eat, so off the two of them went, downstairs to the cafeteria—leaving her alone and already getting hungry—in the labor room wearing nothing but her hospital nightie. They made sure the nurses took her clothes so she wouldn't be heading to the snack machines—so apparently she was already under suspicion.

And wouldn't you know it? Her contractions stopped. But our Vickie decided, contractions or not, she had had herself enough of this business and she was ready to get this thing *done*. They had put the little band thingee around her belly that measures contractions, so every few minutes, she would squeeeeeezee her stomach really tight and hold it for a little bit—in what she thought was a pretty good imitation of a genuine contraction—so that weird little measurements appeared on the screen. When the doctor came back—after lunch—he took a look and said, well, he didn't think they were really contractions, but *something* was obviously going on—so he went and did the C-section. When baby Sam weighed in at eight pounds, Vickie was sooo relieved. All she could think of—after she set this ruse in irrevocable motion—was what if he was tiny and underweight, and she had faked her contractions largely because she was hungry? I say, all's well that ends well and all that—especially if it ends with *snacks*.

Igmo Husbands

From the title of this chapter, don't you just *know* it's gonna be at least half the book?

I can only speak to delivery by surgical means, but I can tell you it was a highly satisfactory experience for me personally. Queen Christine—as fine an example of complete honesty as I can show you—told me that whenever she heard women saying they didn't want an epidural for their deliveries she'd tell 'em she not only wanted an epidural to *have* her babies—she wanted one to *conceive* them. And I know she's sincere about that.

But sooner or later—however we get 'em here, whatever pain and indignities we must suffer in the process—once they're here it's like none of that ever happened. All we can see or think about is that precious face. That perfect angel.

Of course, from time to time, something else besides our

baby's perfection does register in our consciousness—the fact that our husbands occasionally engage in behavior that indelibly marks them as complete and total igmos.

Sometimes this is made manifest very early on. I was told of one husband who apparently had some limited experience with puppies and kittens but had clearly never seen a brand-new human before, since he asked if babies are born with their eyes open.

A nurse I know had just found out she was pregnant and shared the happy news with her husband, Rodney. The next morning, while she was taking a bath, Rodney became hysterical because he was afraid the baby would drown. I'm not sure if he's improved much with time. I do know that when they went to the hospital to deliver the baby, he could not understand why she wasn't packing the little spoon and fork set they'd been given at the baby shower—*how was she going to feed the baby?*

Ole Rod might be one of those guys who's no Einstein—or even Einstein's dumb brother—but he's probably simple enough to deal with—you know some of these—they've basically got two gears—Horny and Hungry. So if he comes into the room *without* a hard-on, you know to hand him a sandwich. (My seester, Judy, and I have determined that our own two life positions are Hungry and Sleepy. Anything that happens pretty much just makes us hungry, and once we get that taken care of, then we're sleepy. Occasionally, something will happen to make us crabby—but that's usually just if something interferes with our sleeping and/or eating.)

Scholarly books about child rearing usually offer the same lame advice about Expectant Fathers and how, much like a small child who learns his mother is pregnant again, they're liable to feel "left out" and generally pitiful in a hundred or so other ways and how special care must be taken to soothe them and help them to rise above this. Oh, boofuckinghoo. I think Queen Shauna whacked that ole nailhead a good 'un with this little nugget directed at her own erstwhile errant husband: "Just because your mama raised you to be a spoiled brat and to think the world revolves around you don't make it SO," thus indicating to him her rock-solid expectation that he was gonna be growin' on up pretty quick like.

Just as many devoted husbands experience morning sickness and other pregnancy-related maladies, presumably out of sympathy and empathy for their wives, I think it's possible that pregnancy causes a good many of them to simply lose their minds, just as we do, at least temporarily.

Queen Julie—who was not, amazingly, writing to me from a prison while serving a life sentence for murder—said that, with her first child, her month-early onset of labor inconveniently coincided with her husband's golf game with a few of his cousins. The golf pro went out and hunted them down on the course and advised Igmo of the impending early birth of his first child, and he said, of course, that he was *so* on his way right that very second. Now, the golf course in question was situated only about forty-five minutes away from the hospital, so when Igmo arrived some three hours later, he pleaded, "Heavy traffic." Early Baby did come on that day and was, thankfully, fine. It was not until the one-year birthday party for Early Baby that Julie discovered the truth about Igmo's lengthy trek to the hospital that day. It spewed forth between guffaws from those golfing cousins that after her frantic phone call was received and the promise to hit the road immediately was made, it happened that a good many more holes of golf were played on account of one of those golfing cousins was a daddy already and he said it was a known fact that first babies always take forever to actually show up. They would have played the whole course but it started *lightning* and it scared them off.

If you ask me, it's a wonder they weren't all *struck*.

Queen Tammy had been having contractions five minutes apart for what seemed like forever and the doctor suggested she might want to walk around the halls a bit to . . . well, who knows what for—my guess is to make room in the bed for her husband to take a *nap* because that's what happened. We can only surmise that her own preoccupation with the protracted labor pains is all that prevented her from performing Pillow Therapy on that napping husband so that he might sleep forever in heavenly peace.

Queen Jan was in labor for about twenty-four hours with her first child and her (then) husband stood by and fed her—in

Jan's words—"those blankety-blank-blank *ice chips* they think we need when we're in labor." Jan clearly was not appreciative of the ice chips nor of her (then) husband's feeding them to her. But she didn't cross the line over into wanting him to *die* until he left her side to go across the street to have a *beer* and get himself a big giant corned beef *sandwich* which he then brought into the room where she lay laboring—even to her very bedside he brought it—where he stood and *ate* the whole entire thing. It was twenty-three years ago and even divorcing him was not quite enough to quell her fury. The smell of corned beef still makes her want to go to the gun show.

I have heard from any number of women whose husbands' *only* concern upon arrival at the hospital with their laboring wives was not, as you might assume (you being a right-thinking *woman*, of course), for getting their laboring wives comfortably on a gurney and safe in the capable hands of medical personnel—but rather for *obtaining a good parking spot.* I cannot tell you how many women I know who nearly gave birth alone on the sidewalk outside an emergency room after being practically shoved out the car door onto the pavement by a husband literally crazed by the sight of a nearby vacant parking place and another car that would surely beat him to it if he didn't get over there *right now.* Surely this is some form of temporary insanity? When a dear friend of mine, near tears, described this exact same scenario from her own first child's birth, I came up with a theory—not so much out of any real belief in her husband's inner goodness as a genuine desire to say *something, anything* that would offer a comforting explanation to my friend for her suffering at the hands of her most loved one.

I postulated that Men Like to Feel in Control of Situations — and if there was ever a deal where they have *zero* control, it would have to be in a labor-and-delivery-type situation. They played a crucial role in the kickoff of the game, but they've been sidelined ever since. You, their beloved wife, are in obvious excruciating pain and Something Major Is Under Way and, well, if you Google "Shit-or-Go-Blind Situations for Men," this pops up pretty high on the list. So they are *desperate for something* they can be 100 percent on top of, something they can handle efficiently, something they *know* how to do — and all that readily presents itself is Parking the Fucking Car — so there you go.

If it saves the life of one Igmo husband at least long enough to give him the opportunity to redeem his sorry ass, well, then I suppose it was worth the semi-lie to my friend. And, truth be told, Queen Julie's sorry-ass husband *did* redeem himself many times over in the years to come — so, fine.

Queen Jessica's husband, Wayne, was right there with her every step of the way, paying attention, being sympathetic, rubbing her back, and just generally making himself readily available for being held accountable for every spasm of pain she experienced. Gotta love him for all that. But when they finally went to the hospital to have the baby, he dutifully and lovingly got her set up with the proper nursing staff *without regard to the parking situation,* and as they took her away, they left him with instructions as to where he should go to get suited up in his scrubs before heading to the delivery room. Well, he didn't come and he didn't come and nobody could believe that he could be such a stand-up guy all the way through this thing only to weasel out at the last minute. So Jessica's actual *doctor* left her to go on the Wayne Hunt, and he found him, too, in a total panic wad, frantically searching in vain for scrubs in the janitor's closet. Bless his little heart.

If there's nothing we can do to really prepare *ourselves* for the marvels and atrocities of pregnancy and childbirth—what hope is there for a poor old *guy*? I mean really. Bless their hearts. Queen Ellie reported to me that her best friend, Sharon, said that her sweet husband, Jack, did try his dead-level best to be what he imagined was "supportive," and to his credit, he was there for the whole entire birth, but when the OB came in to check on her progress, she called for Jack to come around to the nether end of the bed for a doc's-eye view of the whole situation. Sharon reported that his eyes got enormous and he crept back up by her head and, leaning down, whispered into her ear, "Shar, there is absolutely *nothin'* down there that I recognize."

It is fairly shocking and somewhat appalling and I am considerably dismayed by the number of women who have reported to me that their husbands expected them to conceive and/or deliver their offspring on a rigidly set schedule—said schedule being one developed by the husband, of course, with a nod to the IRS. Yes, *more than one* husband has demanded that conception be accomplished no later than the end of the first quarter of the year to ensure that delivery of the child could be taken in time for that year's tax return, and if conception failed to occur within the specified time allotted, the whole thing would have to be shelved until the following year. Really.

And at least two women reported that, as their previously husband-approved end-of-year due dates approached, their respective husbands had actually said out loud to the obstetricians that if it appeared for any reason that the baby involved would be attempting to remain in utero through the last day of December, he (the husband) wanted an induction scheduled in a timely fashion to protect his precious deduction. Having heard it all before, the not-surprised-but-nonetheless-disgusted docs chose to respond as if the creepy husbands were joking, which did not entertain the creeps at all.

There is much talk—regarding teenagers—about "making adult choices" before one is ready—physically, emotionally, financially—to handle the consequences. Yoo-hoo! Hel-lo-o-o! Supposedly grown-up me-e-enfolks! This applies to you, to-o-o!

You should know—and accept—*before* you commence starting up babies in folks that not only do babies come pretty much when they get good and ready but the doctors involved in the process *do* expect to be paid in full—before the most important part of the services are even rendered, satisfactorily or otherwise. You cannot shop around—as one poor Queen's husband demanded she do—for a more economical alternative whose payment would be due upon receipt of the merchandise, in good condition, with all the parts working (and the "factory" all cleaned up and restored to its original condition). Well, I suppose you can shop around for whatever the hell you want to—but lemme know if and when you *find* it.

Oh, and if it turns out that your wife needs an emergency C-section, you really don't want to start your own video of the blessed event with the sound of your own voice saying, "Oh, great, here we are in surgery. I can't believe you put me through all those stupid natural-childbirth classes for nothing! What a total waste of time and money!"

And apparently it does *not* go without saying, in some households shared by women and men, that no, a *carpet sweeper* is not considered to be a welcome or on any level even acceptable First Mother's Day gift, even if it does provide us with the means to clean without making enough noise to wake the baby. So there, we've said it—don't do that, igmo.

On rare occasions, we show our own igmo sides—I said it was rare. But Queen G-Louise had been in labor for two whole days, and after two hours of steady pushing, she propped up and told her labor nurse that she thought she was just gonna go on home and rest awhile—she promised she'd be back tomorrow, first thing, to finish up, but she was done for today. Now, had G-Louise been a lady HORSE instead of a lady person, this could have been an option for her. Yes, my horsey friends tell me that right up until the third stage of delivery, a mare can stop the whole show if she decides something about the arrangement doesn't quite suit her—say, for instance, her igmo foal-daddy has just come by the stall and said something irritating about a tax credit or brought her a stupid carpet sweeper. Alas, G-Louise didn't have to shut up necessarily—but she did have to go on and put up.

I myownself had a close encounter of the igmo kind when my precious darlin' BoPeep was born to me and the ineffable MoonPie. It was deep in the night after she was yanked from my severed midsection and I was enjoying an even deeper sleep—afforded me by massive doses of most excellent drugs and the in-bed peeing ease of my catheter—when I was suddenly roused from my slumber by a fierce and extremely loud yowling emanating from the tiny crib across the room—more specifically, from the tiny baby inside the tiny crib across the room.

MoonPie was ensconced, snoring on a decibel level competitive with the yowling, on the cot that lay between me and the yowler, so even if I had not been tethered by my handy plumbing device, I could not, having been cut half in two only a few hours earlier, made an easy jump of it in order to see to the needs of the new girl in the room. She was yowling in ever-increasing crescendos and his snoring was matching the increase at every level.

I began by whispering and hissing at him in my efforts to roust him, and, of course, nobody could hear me over the yowl/snore duet, so I was eventually forced to summon up and hurl a pretty substantial holler in his direction that, coupled with a smartly aimed pillow, did the trick. Sort of. "Whuh—what? What is it?" he asked, brilliantly. "Ahhh, you wanna check on her?" "*WHO?!*" I swear before God, he asked me, "Who?" And so, with all the scraps of patience I had left to my name, I replied, "Well, you might wanna *start* with the one *screaming* over there!"

Of course, this is the same man I was married to three months later when the *tree* fell on the house and literally landed *in* the bedroom, *on* the bed, immediately next to where I lay sleeping with the sleeping three-month-old BoPeep in her bassinette right next to me. It landed, actually, smack-dab in the middle of what would have been *him* had he not fallen asleep on the sofa in the den. But this same man, being some-how miraculously awakened by the sound of the eighty-foot pine tree crashing through the roof and into our bedroom, which was all the way down the hall from where he was sleep-ing, so, as I said, it was a miracle he heard it at all, but he did, sprang up to run to the door of the bedroom and shout in to me, *"You were only dreaming!"* As I clasped BoPeep to my heaving bosom, weeping with gratitude that she was unharmed, I plucked pine bark off my pillow, and thought, "No, I was *dreaming* you were here beside me."

No, not really—that dream wasn't to come until years later.

The igmonosity of some men lives on long after they are dead and gone. I met the most delightful young woman at a Lit-erary Fest outside Chicago—Queen Shauna—when she made

41

a beeline for me after my session to share with me this touching story about her grandparents. A huge family reunion had been held to celebrate the ninety-sixth birthday of the matriarch of the clan. It was a sight to behold—with all her children and all forty of her grandkids gathered around her reverently. They asked her to tell them what their dear old departed grandfather had been like and they waited in respectful silence for her reply, which was, "Annnnh, all he ever wanted to do was drink beer and screw me." I wished that I had her for my own grandma.

Oh, but every now and again, a Dream Boy comes along—a true Spud Stud. Hearing about Queen Suzie's husband is what keeps every other woman in the world out there hunting for one—just like him. When Queen Suzie was expecting her first child, she and The Man Among Men had several well-meaning friends who shared their thirty-six-hour-labor-with-failed-epidural stories—very off-putting as we all know, but it was about six or eight months too late for Suzie to change her mind or anything. By way of cheering her up and giving her something to focus on besides her stark terror, the darlin' man told Suzie that if she was in labor for under six hours, he would go Big Joory shopping! And sure enough—she will always believe it's because she was steady thinking about sparklies coming her way—she was in labor for only two hours and she wore a new tennis bracelet home from the hospital. I think Diamonds on Delivery is just an excellent policy.

How to Talk to a Pregnant Woman

There is all kinds of stuff that you just shouldn't ask *any* woman. Directly. If you want to know something personal about her, ask her nail technician or somebody who went to high school with her. You can find out just about anything you want to know about her this way—especially if she's a bad tipper or was prone to stealing ninth-grade boyfriends.

Under most circumstances, it is considered impolite to ask a woman her age. As much as I do love a bargain, I feel certain that sales have suffered due to the Senior Citizen Discount offered in department stores. Oh, it's not the discount itself that's the problem—it's great to *get* a discount—anytime, for any reason. It's the way it's presented. Timing—and sometimes volume—can be everything. I do know of women who have literally walked away in a huff, without completing their purchase, just leaving the stuff piled by the register, when the perky twentysomething salesgirl remarked a little too loudly, *"You know, you get a Senior Citizen Discount on everything you buy today!"* That's right. I know women who would really rather *pay more* than admit publicly that they are over fifty. Perhaps the stores would do better to take the suggestion of Queen Katrinka and call it the "Hot Babe Discount." They'd prolly line up to buy *extra* stuff just to have that hollered out at the checkout stand.

I, for one, have never minded the age issue. There are so *many* things in my life about which I am mildly chagrined, if not out-and-out ashamed of, things for which I and I alone am completely responsible, and I hope you don't ask me about any of *those* things. But the fact that I am fifty-four and climbing is not my fault—ain't nothin' I can do to stop it, 'cept *die,* and most days I'm not ready to do that. I've never seen the point in lying about it—there's only so much even the best plastic surgeon can do, and in my opinion, hair dye just looks silly. At some point, it does stop fooling anybody and it's just kinda pathetic to hang on to being blond (or brunette or redheaded) when you can hardly hang on to your walker. And unless you're an absolute orphan and have changed your name and moved to Nebraska, *somebody* out there *knows* how old you are and, boy hidee, will they ever be tickled to death to *tell* it, especially if they find out you're mincing around, lying about it.

And who cares how old you are anyway? I've got *waaaay*

more interestin' stuff to lie about in *my* life, thank you very much. For instance, don't ask me where I got the Spring Hill College baseball T-shirt. (That's just a little special dig at my husband, The Cutest Boy in the World—on account of I've got this Spring Hill College baseball T-shirt—that I got under Completely Innocent Circumstances—but when he asked me about it once, it caught me off-guard and so I *looked* guilty and he ragged me about it—so *now*, it's a Big Deal that I will *not*, under any circumstances, discuss the Spring Hill College baseball T-shirt and how I came to be in possession of it. It's good for him. Keeps him alert. I keep it buried in my closet, and once every six or eight months, I dig it up and come out wearing it—with nary a word—it's huge fun.)

It's never really a good idea to discuss weight—even amongst nonpregnant womenfolk. Well, if everybody's kinda the same size, we can all commiserate—while we eat a pie—and that's fine, but if everybody's "normal-sized" but you—you just keep your skinny little mouth shut. Especially if you're something ridiculous like a size 0—because the rest of us will be talking behind your back and arguing whether or not we would need to put your feet in concrete in order to keep your bony ass on the bottom of the river we will fling you into after we force-feed you a pie or if you'd just sink okay on your own—since there ain't much to you but elbows and shins—you not being bothered with any especially buoyant parts like tits or ass.

In the presence of pregnant women, this is a definite sleeping dog that should be left a-snooze—nothing good can come from bringing it up. Because either the pregnant one doubled her body weight in the first six months and is sure to hit the triple by the time she hits the finish line and she does not want to even *think* about it, let alone talk about it, *or* she's one of *those*—who's gained only a pound and a half and is still wearing her normal clothes—while doing her first triathlon—at the end of the eighth month—and every other woman there, whose pregnancy was much more like the first woman's, will want to bury her alive in onion rings and red velvet cake just to shut her up.

If, however, the hefty one brings it up herownself and freely discloses to one and all that she now outweighs her husband by sixty-two pounds, it is the responsibility of every other person present—be they female, male, or uncommitted—to look aghast and express utter disbelief that such a thing is true—why, she just looks like the tiniest little ole bit of nuthin'!—she is just makin' that *up*—she could not possibly have gained more than seven pounds at the very most—she should just hush that silly talk right this second—and so on and so forth. The crowd should be prepared to keep up a steady stream of these lies until it becomes evident that the clear and present danger has passed. One indication that it might be safe to sound the "all clear" would be when the little behemoth heaves herself up to waddle over for one more pass at the buffet line. Bless her heart.

Most women cannot be safely queried on the subject of "work." Oh, you can ask 'em about their *jobs* all day long— what I meant was "work" as in "have you had any *Work* done?" This is another one I'm cool with personally. Is there anybody out there who *doesn't* know I've had my eyes done *and* a full face-lift? (For details, go read my earlier books—I do tell it all, sistahs!) I was thrilled to get it all done and I'm tickled to death to talk about it—so if you're dying to know something—fire away—e-mail me at hrhjill@sweetpotatoqueens.com and I'll answer you, I promise.

But I encounter all manner of women who will, when the subject of plastic surgery comes up—as it always does in any gathering of women that lasts more than fifteen minutes— freeze and look so much like a Botoxed deer in the headlights that you almost expect to hear a big *whump* as they get tossed up on the hood of the car. It's pretty fun to watch, actually. Every- body in the room already *knows* she's had Work done—because she's got that too-tight-ponytail pull going on and she looks kinda like a reflection in a car fender—but when we start talk- ing—just in general terms—about plastic surgery—she gets all shifty-eyed (even Botox can't hide lyin' eyes) and guilty- looking and she starts tap-dancing around the subject—trying desperately to *change* it—to anything else—ASAP.

It's pretty fun, in a mean sorta way (and isn't that just the best sometimes—be honest), to let her change the subject then watch her carefully applied cosmetics start to puddle up in the sweat as you just keep bringing it back around to plastic surgery again and again.

It's generally best not to ask a woman about her husband's latest fling unless she brings it up first. That ole saw about killing messengers was not, after all, completely unfounded in fact. And definitely do not participate in roundtable discussions regarding the preferred methods for killing him or anything else about which you could be called to testify in the not-too-distant future. If this topic seems unavoidable, make certain to speak in euphemisms so that you can truthfully swear that all the two of you ever talked about was rodent removal and the chipping of dead tree limbs.

Okay, all that applies to pretty much any woman in the world who is *not* pregnant. There are some additional rules when it comes to conversing with women who are with child. (Not to be confused with women who are merely accompanied by children. "With child" definitely means the child is with her—but on the *inside*. And do not think for one second that that did not need to be explained to *some igmo* out there.)

Talking to pregnant women is a crapshoot on a good day, but there is one absolute rule that is clad in solid iron forevermore. What would be higher up the totem pole than a Cardinal Rule? Pope Rule? Whatever—this one is *the* highest, *the* biggest—the One That Must Never Be Broken at Any Time Ever by Anybody: Never, for any reason, *ask* a woman if she is pregnant. I don't care if she's sticking out to the middle of the room and her belly button looks like it's about to launch itself into orbit at any moment—simply tell her she looks "amazing" and let her take the lead. **Do *not* ask the question.** This is 100 percent WRONG every time—on so many levels.

Right off the bat, there's the at least fifty-fifty chance that she's *not,* and it does not matter one bit the circumstances contributing to this nonstate of pregnancy—you, the asker, are screwed. Maybe she just had a baby yesterday—or last month—or last year—or eighteen years ago—and thus is not pregnant at this particular moment in time that *you* chose to indirectly tell her that she *looks pregnant.* Or maybe she has never been pregnant or even entertained the idea of it in her whole entire *life,* including this moment. You have not endeared yourself to her. Because it's not just an idle question designed to spark a conversation—like, "Do you tango?" Asking another person about her gestation status carries with it at least the implication that there is some visible reason for the question, and it can create an uncomfortable social situation for all concerned.

Perhaps she's been trying for years to get pregnant with no success, or worse—perhaps she just suffered a miscarriage. In any event, you have not embarked on a happy note with her.

If she is, in fact, pregnant but "just a little bit"—not really to the sticking-out-to-there, belly-button-popping stage—and you ask her, she is then forced to wonder if everybody else in the world is staring at her and asking themselves, "Is that girl pregnant or is she just fat and misshapen?"

Here's a tip: If, judging from appearances alone, you are pretty sure that the woman is, in fact, pregnant, it would be best for all concerned—indeed, for the world at large—if you just didn't ask her *anything* besides what you could do for her at that moment, especially if you are a man. Because if she is, in fact, pregnant, there is no way to tell at first glance just where on the broad spectrum of possibilities her *hormones* might be lurking at that moment (waiting to pounce on the unsuspecting), and thus any question asked (even the proffering of services, truth be told) is likely to be met with a surprising response. I say surprising because, on a given day, during just about any pregnancy, the slightest occurrence can and most likely will be met with a response (from the pregnant one) that totally negates what was heretofore thought to be a fairly immutable law of physics: Newton's Third Law—which states that for every action there is an equal and opposite *re*-action.

I snort as I read that and can only assume that either Newton was childless or he was out of town a whole lot. Nobody who's ever been pregnant or who's ever known a pregnant woman would put any stock whatsoever in Newton's Third Law. As a matter of fact, I think I speak for all pregnant or formerly pregnant women when I say, "Newton can bite my ass and stuff that Third Law up his own."

It is not only possible—I'd say there's an extremely high probability that there will be, at some point in any pregnancy, an "action" that wouldn't slosh a full glass of tea in the Real

World but will get a *"re*-action" in Pregnant World that breaks every glass in the county and endangers the tea crop of the whole world while singeing the eyebrows off an errant but possibly well-meaning husband and/or baby-daddy.

Queen Beth and her husband are both licensed professional counselors who were only about six months into their marriage and their careers in the mental-health field when she got pregnant. She shared this with me—in order that I might share it with y'all—just so you can see that Education really doesn't improve them all that much. Guys, I mean. At the point in her pregnancy when her girth prevented her from fitting into a booth at the Pizza Inn, Beth's hormones were also not surprisingly at their zenith—and there was much turbulence as the "squall line" moved through the room. (Meaning that Beth was flouncing around and squalling a whole lot.) And the Igmo Though Highly Educated Husband said to her—out loud, out of his own igmo mouth—"You know, you would feel so much better if you would replace your negative thinking with positive, rational thoughts." Oh, my. Too bad there wasn't a video of this little scene—I'm sure it would have instantly become standard curriculum in all college psychology classes as *proof* that Cognitive Behavioral Therapy does *not* work on big giant pregnant women.

It would also make a pretty good demonstration for What Instant Remorse Looks Like on the Face of an Igmo Though Highly Educated Husband. Don't you just *know* he was wishing he could snatch those words back outta the air and cram them down his own throat, along with his severed and shredded tongue—which is, I am quite sure, a service that Queen Beth provided for him on the spot.

These instructions are all for men, of course—women don't need to be told these things. Even if she's never been pregnant, a woman has at least suffered some form of hormonal angst and had to endure the igmonosity of some guy. So we get it and we can cut whatever slack is needed for our sister—knowing, as we do, that it will pass and all will be well (and also that It Is His Fault, Whatever It Is). We also know that the healing process could be enhanced and expedited greatly if we were allowed to perform human sacrifices or at least the occasional minor mutilation, but no—the patriarchal society in which we live denies us even the simplest remedies. Sigh. It is the well from whence our empathy springs.

Past Your Due Date?

You're three weeks past your due date and the novelty of being pregnant wore off about thirty weeks ago. You only have that one pair of sweatpants and size 10X T-shirt that you can fit in and that's just fine with you. You now totally understand how it is that bugs and turtles can die just from winding up on their backs. You haven't seen your feet in a couple of months—the only way you can see them is in a full-length mirror. Which is also the only way you can see your belly button that now looks like an auxiliary nose. Your underwear looks like pillowcases, your bras like colanders.

Everyone you encounter—whether you know them or not—feels not only free but compelled to ask you the same question, varying only in their selection of emphasis: "*How* much weight have you gained?" "How *much* weight have you

53

gained?" "How much *weight* have you gained?" "How much weight *have* you gained?" "How much weight have *you* gained?" "How much weight have you *gained*?" But the variation does little to help your feelings—which are genocidal. You wonder when *National Geographic* will be calling to schedule your naked portrait.

On the rare occasions when you leave the house, everyone you meet, after they have gotten the burning query about your weight out of the way, then goes directly to the next most important—although even less intelligent—question, and that is—every fourth-trimester woman's favorite—*"Haven't you had that baby yet?"*

That puts me in mind of a Queen I met in Wichita—we'll call her "Tammy" just because we do like that name—who had herself a grand time at Wal-Mart at the expense of a woman—not of even the most casual acquaintance—who asked Tammy a question for which she was not even entitled to an answer—and boy, did she ever get more than she bargained for.

Tammy had a baby girl about eight months old. Tammy's sister had a baby girl about four months old and sis had to return to work quickly, so Tammy volunteered to babysit every day. Tammy was quite the active young thing at the time, so it was nothing for her to put one baby on her back and the other in a stroller and just hit the trail for whatever errands needed running. Folks were always noticing how close in age the babies appeared to be and commenting and Tammy was generally too busy to fool with them.

So one day, a woman came charging up to Tammy and asked her how far apart her babies were and Tammy just told her, "Four months," and proceeded to walk on by. The woman stood there, dumbfounded, for a second, and then she fell in pursuit. "Four months?" Tammy kept walking. "Yep." The woman could not help herself. *"Four months?"* So Tammy stopped pushing the stroller and turned to the woman and said, "Yes, it is most unusual, I admit— but I have a double uterus and I got pregnant in both of 'em, four months apart, so there's only four months' difference in their ages."

"Why, I have never heard of such a thing!" the woman gasped—totally hooked on the bullshit line, and our Tammy, she never even let up. "Oh, I know. You just hardly ever hear of it happening with humans—it's pretty common with cattle but not in human beings. It was extremely rare." Tammy musta talked to that woman for twenty minutes, telling her every minute detail of her two simultaneous pregnancies, and she never told her any different.

That was thirty years ago and we figger that woman is still telling people about the day she met the girl in Wal-Mart with the two uteruses.

So, if you're three weeks past your due date and some fool asks you, "Haven't you had that baby yet?" you just look 'em square in the eye and tell 'em, "Oh, mercy, yes, I had the *first* one, she's out in the car—it ain't so awful hot out, do you think?

This is the *second* one—in my *other* uterus—and it's not due for another month yet—but thanks for asking!"

So anyway—you're as good as ten months pregnant and you and your Igmo Husband go to what surely to *God* will be your last visit before you have this *baby,* and he, so helpfully, asks the doctor if there is not something to be done to help bring on the labor. The doctor suggests that orgasms might help, and Igmo says, "For me or for her?" And he was dead-ass serious. Fortunately, your fingers are far too swollen to pull a trigger.

Queen Cindy was in labor for forty-nine hours—her sister thinks she should just round up to fifty—who's gonna argue with a woman who labored for more than two whole days? Cindy has never been able to come up with *anything* funny about her extremely long labor. Her best friend agrees with her, adding, "I wouldn't want to do something that felt *good* for forty-nine hours." True that, friend girl.

There Are Already Plenty of George Foremans

It's an awesome responsibility, giving another creature a name — I will ponder for days and weeks over just the right name for a new dog or cat — knowing that I'll be uttering that name tens of thousands of times in the coming years, no doubt with varying degrees of emotion and volume. To contemplate assigning a lifelong handle to another human being should render one sleepless for at least a night or two — I beg you to give serious consideration to the long-term effects your choice potentially holds for your precious child. Be assured, your child will appreciate your thoughtfulness.

Little Alexis, who's about ten years old now, just loves — as most children do — to hear stories about when she was a baby and when her mama was expecting her and pretty much any and all things concerning her. Curious about what might have been, she asked her mama what the other options had been when the time came to choose her name. Mama replied that, well, she had been "pretty much up for anything." This did not sit well with Alexis, who hotly informed her mama, "You're 'pretty much up for anything' when you're goin' out to *eat—not* when you're tryin' to name your *child*!"

Former world heavyweight boxing champion George Foreman spared not a moment's effort when his five sons came along. He simply named all five of them "George Foreman." So you should probably consider the market pretty well saturated with that particular name.

And be very wary about the assignation of nicknames. Yes, it's entertaining for *you* and the other adults when the child is an infant, but I'm telling you, those names are quite adhesive and it may prove quite difficult to remove them when the novelty has worn off.

I don't know if truly dreadful nicknames really are more the provenance of the South or if my readers in other parts of the country have just been lax about sharing the wealth of their states' silly sobriquets. A most excellent reference source for Southern "noms de knuckleheads" is the book *Southern Fried Divorce,* which was written, of course, by my very own seester, Judy Conner. She's got several solid pages of nothing but hideous nicknames—gleaned from obituaries. Do not let that escape your attention: These appalling appellations followed these hapless individuals *all the way to the grave,* and they were included prominently in what was likely the very last public writing concerning them and their lives.

Do you *really* want your child's listing in the high school yearbook to bear witness to the fact that, as an infant, you labeled the little darling something regrettable like "Dogboy," "Koochie," "Moochie," "Poochie," "Squinchy," "Squeeky," or "Lightbulb"—just to name a very few of the apparently endless and equally awful possibilities?

I'll tell you that my very own mother—who was, in fact, born a Yankee but has devoted herself for the last sixty-some-odd years to overcoming it—was always horrified by what she considered to be the "Southern" nicknaming proclivities—especially as they applied to babies and, more important, to *grandparents*. So when Judy produced the first beloved grandchild and named him "James Trevor," and Mother would tease Judy by referring to him as "Jimmy T," Judy gave her ample warning that should this name-calling persist, Mother would soon find herself being addressed by the most loathed and dreaded "MAWMAW." Mother thought the whole "Jimmy T" joke, and the discomfiture it brought to my sister, oh, just so amusing.

Trevor is now in his forties and has *never* been called "Jimmy T" by anyone *other* than my teasing mother—however, she and my father were known far and wide as "MawMaw" and "PawPaw." Over the years, even their own personal friends began to call them "MawMaw" and "PawPaw." Until Daddy died in 1982, they even called *each other* "MawMaw" and "Paw-

Paw." So watch out with the nickname business—it may bite you in the ass.

As it did the husband of my friend Quita—pardon me, ex-husband. He was so bad to make up names for their children, and, try as she might, Quita could never induce him to stop it. He called the baby boy "Blondie Dagwood," he called their daughter "Tubby Tub-Tank" (he *is* the ex, as I said), and the eldest child was dubbed "John Anthony Buzzard Nuts." The origin of these names remains a mystery.

They moved to the ex's small rural hometown just in time for big brother to begin the first grade. The first day of school, Quita took her young son to his classroom and was pleased to discover that his teacher was a woman she recognized from church as an old friend of ex's family. Teacher greeted them both warmly and turned to the small class of around fifteen tiny pupils and said, "Boys and girls, we have a new student today." She then asked him to tell the class his name, and he just grinned his winningest grin at them all as he announced loudly that his name was *"John Anthony Buzzard Nuts."*

A cursory glance around her told Quita that there was not a single solitary hole in the entire room into which she might crawl, so she just gave her boy a squeeze and told him to have a great day and she'd pick him up that afternoon. From thence she betook herself to the field where the future ex was farming something or other, whereupon she summoned him and most firmly invited him to meet Jesus.

6

Baby Food

The Sweet Potato Queens were born in 1982. My precious Tater Tot, BoPeep, came along in 1988, and there was never any doubt in my mind as to her Queenly Potential. The child's first two-syllable word was "titties"—we breast-fed for quite a while—and her second one was "bubbles," as in Tiny. Priorities firmly in place from the get-go—Food, followed closely by Frivolity.

Breast-feeding was just about the greatest job I ever had, and one of the best things about it, in my opinion, was that nobody else could do it but me. I never minded getting up with her—it was a sacred honor and my deepest joy—really. (It can wear you out, though. I have a photograph of me standing in the hall holding Peep, who is latched on to me like my own little refrigerator magnet, and I look pret-ty tired.) I never even bought a pump — Peep never saw a bottle until I weaned her at twenty-two months, and I did it then only because MoonPie and I were going on a cruise. My mama was going to be taking care of Peep while we were gone, and I thought things would go a lot smoother for both of them if the whole weaning process was behind us before I left. Not to mention the fact that I would have been lactating all over the ship.

Lactating is a phenomenal experience. I had gone my whole *en*-tire premotherhood life with scarcely enough bosom to fill a good-sized thimble, and although there was a substantial size increase during pregnancy, that was dwarfed by the explosion in my bra as I commenced nursing. And speaking of exploding bras, mine sorta did, at least once.

If you've ever breast-fed a baby, you know what I'm talking about — if you haven't, there's really no way to imagine it but try: Your breasts fill *up*. You can feel them filling up — it's like you've got a couple of big water balloons on the front of your body — if they were transparent, I imagine you could watch the levels rise — and no matter where you are or what you're doing, if you're full-up and a baby cries within earshot of you — doesn't even have to be *your* baby — doesn't even have to be *a* baby — anybody can walk up behind you and say, "WA-A-A-AH!" — you are gonna spring a leak.

Only it's not so much a leak as it is a fountain flowing, deep and wide, and this is a tide that cannot be immediately stemmed.

I was at home with BoPeep for the first few months and I

was happy to feed her whenever she indicated she was ready for a little something. When she got herself on a fairly predictable schedule, I went back to teaching classes at the Y and just took her with me. The precious Kate McRaney was a darlin' teenager that summer, and I hired Kate to sit in the ladies' locker room and hold BoPeep for an hour at a time while I taught class. That was her only job — hold the baby. Change her if she needed it and come get me out of class if she cried — since I was the bearer of what would make her stop — and other than that — just hold the baby.

Besides a baby crying, there are at least a couple of other things can cause a lactating mom to "let down" — that's what it's called when your milk is expressed — or the faucets are turned on, as it were. To the uninitiated, "let down" would seem to imply a gentle issuance — like an event almost "oozy" in nature and definitely very slow — but there is nothing slow about it. I'll get to that in a minute.

Warmth induces a letdown — so a hot shower can do it, and also exercise. I was teaching a fairly high-impact aerobics class and all was well as long as I was exercising, but once I stopped jumping around, I would let down. I just kept a towel handy, and when we took to the mats for our cooldown, I would press the towel to my chest until I felt it subside.

My best friend at the Y was the physical director, David. While I was pregnant, David tore his Achilles tendon and was on crutches for a long time. He and I would go out to lunch together nearly every day and we got all manner of special consideration everywhere we went. He was on crutches and I was about fourteen and a half months pregnant—people just assumed we were married and they were *soooo* sympathetic—waited on us most attentively. Enjoying and appreciating the extra service, we just never bothered to inform them that we were only friends.

So anyway, one day David popped into my aerobics class at the height of the workout and motioned from the door that he needed me for something right away. I ran back there—and forgot my towel. Uh-oh. We were walking down the hall and I was starting to feel that telltale tingle that told me my ta-tas were about to trickle—when out of the locker room came Kate carrying the sobbing BoPeep. *Big* uh-oh.

My already ready-to-pop breasts heard that baby and I turned into a dual set of fire hoses. I'm telling you, it didn't just run down the front of my leotard—it shot, from both sides, across the entire hall. I immediately clasped my hands over them, and it was just as if I had put my hands over gushing water faucets—it spewed out in all directions—I swear you could *hear* it. David was totally freaking out—*"Omigod!! What are you gonna do?! What are you gonna do?! Omigod! Omigod!"* Bless his heart. I'm sure he was scarred for life.

Breast-feeding worked just great for us. It doesn't for some folks, but for us it was plenty swell. As I said, I enjoyed the exclusivity it gave me with the person I adored the most on the planet, plus, as a deeply dedicated lazy-ass person, I loved the fact that there was nothing to prepare and likewise no utensils to wash. I am not nor have I ever been frugal, but you can't beat the price on this deal.

It seems to me that breast-fed babies are easier to feed later on as well. Whatever Mom eats is going to have an effect on how her milk tastes to the bambino. Since the titty-baby is already accustomed to a little variety, this helps foster a more adventuresome spirit as new foods are introduced. But since formula is going to taste exactly the same every time, all the time, anything different will be a big surprise to the bottle-baby.

My dear friend the Precious Darlin' George obtained for me a copy of the most excellent child-rearing book, *The Care and Feeding of Children—A Catechism for the Use of Mothers and Children's Nurses*, written by L. Emmett Holt, M.D., first published in 1894. The copy that George found for me was updated in 1917, and it reads a whole lot like the old Betty Crocker stuff. I only wish I'd had a copy when BoPeep was a wee babe. The whole thing is written in a question-and-answer format, making for a very easy and entertaining read.

Question: What (besides a "simple, generous diet"—thanks, Doc!) is important in the life of the nursing mother? In Dr. Holt's opinion, she should lead a simple, natural life—which would include regular out-of-door exercise as soon after her "confinement" as her "condition" will permit. The preferred forms of exercise listed are walking and driving. Driving? How come nobody ever told me that driving was an acceptable form of exercise? How far do I have to drive to lose a pound, I wonder?

The next thing on his list of important stuff in the life of nursing moms—and I assume he's listing stuff by order of importance and priority—is regular movements from the bowels daily. I don't know of anyone for whom number 2 is not a desirable and worthwhile goal; however, he offers no helpful hints for finding the TIME in which to perform this highly desirable and worthwhile function, and for a new mother, nursing or otherwise, this can be a major obstacle. Most days, she's lucky if she can make time for number 1.

The good doctor feels it's very important for the new mommy to go to bed early, and he's pretty emphatic about her lying down for *at least* one hour in the middle of the day. For that statement alone, if Dr. Holt were still alive today, I think I could safely make him the SPQ™ Promise on behalf of all of us without fear of contradiction from any mother anywhere. How do we go about nominating him for sainthood? I would lie down and light a candle to him every afternoon—Dr. Holt, Patron Saint of Naps for the Perpetually Weary Mother.

For nonnursing mothers there was a whole big lot of work to be done—most of it involving *cows*. It was assumed that if you were not nursing, you would be feeding your infant cow's milk—from your own personal cow—and thus you would need to know all about the importance of keeping that stable clean and also sterilizing the milk cans. Once you got the milk out of the cow and into the house, the work was hardly over. You were expected to strain the milk through several thicknesses of cheesecloth and then put it into pre-sterilized half-pint bottles and then run those down to the creek and put them quite up to their necks in the cold water. I guess you'd be wagging that baby with you every step of the way as well. I suppose this could be counted toward your daily exercise—instead of the driving—but it's bound to screw you outta that midday nap.

Trick Them While You Can

If you're concerned that your baby might be a dumbass (I mean, the Igmo Dad gene factor has to be considered here), here's a little test I devised. It gave me solid proof that not only was BoPeep not a dumbass, she was clearly gifted.

First, I allowed her to keep the stray Hershey's Kiss her little eagle eyes spied on the coffee table. It was her Virgin Chocolate Experience and she's never forgotten it—we never do. I helped her unwrap it and together we marveled at its delightful teepee shape—but not for long. She gave it a little sniff and, finding its odor to be irresistible, popped it into her mouth almost immediately, whereupon her little eyes rolled back in her head and she emitted the most protracted and 100 percent sincere sounding *"MMMMMMMMMMMMM"* I believe I've ever heard—before or since—from a person of any age regarding any physical experience. Happy-happy-happy, she was.

Later that same day, having had such a positive adventure with new foods, she willingly put a morsel of boiled okra into that same happy little mouth and immediately burst into tears. So there you have it—my baby is *not* a dumbass. Having this possibility ruled out is always such a relief to any parent.

Of course, some kids are terminal picky eaters from the beginning, no matter what you do, but for even the most intrepid eaters, sampling a few nontasty items can make them reluctant to continue venturing into new edible territories. If you don't want to spend the rest of your life cooking nothing but hamburgers and frozen French fries and having to make "special" spaghetti sauce with no onions or green peppers in it (which means it's not "spaghetti" sauce at all—it's just "tomato" sauce), you're going to have to get creative about tricking them.

I think it's important to get them over that picky-eater crap before sending them out into the world—like to kindergarten. There is nothing more irritating than a picky eater. The whole world hates a picky eater. Picky eaters are even less popular than vegans, and that is hard to imagine.

Restaurants just *looove* to modify their menus to accommodate the palates of children who don't want *anything* that is actually *on* the menu. The Mom of the Hall Clan told me all her kids were so picky, they practically wouldn't eat anything colored—which pretty much rules out the vegetable kingdom. I am also fond of all the "pale" foods I can think of—potatoes, rice, cheese, etc.—so I understand their taste buds to a certain extent, but this was a bit extreme. When they would order pizza, they would take ten minutes listing all the ingredients that should be "held," until finally one perceptive and chase-cutting waiter stopped them mid-litany and asked, "So, you mean you just want a cracker with cheese?"

Peep has never been finicky, and from first taste, she loved everything except squash and boiled okra. Around age seven, she grew out of the boiled okra thing, and will now also consume squash if there's enough cheese involved. But when she was about four, every other kid we knew had a list of about two and a half things they could be relied upon to eat willingly.

So this is like a genuine tip for tricking picky eaters, and I've never had it fail. Take a look at whatever cartoon they are watching for the 800-millionth time and see what the characters are eating. Say, it's *Popeye.* Then make something that a normal nonpicky kid would eat—say, macaroni and cheese. You put spinach in it (a true picky-eater anathema) and tell them, first of all, that it's only for the grown-ups—there's not enough for them to have any—but it's *Popeye Pie.*

If they're watching *Peter Pan,* put green peas in it and it's *Peter Pan Pie.* They love the alliteration, they love that it's called *pie,* and they *reeeally* love that they're getting to eat *your share* of it. Peep and her friends will *still* ask me to make *Popeye Pie* for them—and they're all in college now.

When *The* movie was *The Land Before Time*, I got the kid down the street to eat *turnip greens* by telling her it was "green food." She ate two heaping piles of them with *corn bread* that I had "made from the bark of the tree that the green food came from." The report of this dietary wild leap was received by the child's mother with about the same level of disbelief she might have expressed had I told her that the little girl was coming home early because she wanted to clean her room—and that she was flying down the street with her newly sprouted wings.

Queen Rosie used a similar trick with her kids. She found she could get them to eat absolutely *anything* if she added "pizza" to the name. So, with the help of a dollop of red sauce and a dab of melted mozzarella, she successfully served them "pizza eggs," "fish pizza," and even "pizza spinach."

A Good Mother is Always Adept at Subterfuge.

Life Is Hard Enough——Pledge Beta

A few thoughts about "types" of mothers. Apparently, researchers with more time and money than their projects are worth have now come up with Official Categories for Moms. It seems we have your dearly demented and overtly overachievers—these would be the *Alpha* Moms. They make their own dirt from scratch and start seedlings for their daughter's pre-K class so the children can begin to learn about organic gardening and exotic lettuces as soon as possible in their educational careers. As room mothers, they show up—early and way too perky for normal people—dressed head to toe in couture, hair and makeup professionally installed, teeth preternaturally white, and all displayed in a constant ear-touching smile. They come through the room like whirling dervishes, and when they stop, the room has been transformed into Disney's Rainforest Café, complete with faux rain and faux wild animals. All the snacks are decorated to look like jungle creatures. If you had hired an event planner to handle this event, it would have been ten thousand dollars, minimum, and taken a staff of fourteen to complete.

Alpha Mom pulled it together last evening when she got home from the nightly after-work spinning class she teaches. She already had the stuff on hand, of course—so it was no trouble to coordinate it after she picked her daughter up from dance, soccer, and Mandarin Chinese lessons. While the whatever-Martha-Stewart-suggests-that-busy-but-gourmet-moms-whip-up-to-delight-their-families was cooking, she assembled the monkey cake (no white flour—no white sugar!) and carved the watermelon boat to hold all the fresh fruit disguised as bugs, and after that, well, it was practically all done. Just a few odds and ends to take care of in the morning before her run to greet the dawn, and she mentally double-checked her stock of tropical decorative items as she monogrammed the family's French toast.

(For some reason, all of that reminds me—Lazy Suzy Bon-Bon's three-year-old granddaughter, Molly, was over at a friend's house, and the mom served the kids cheese and crackers, and little Molly BonBon asked the woman, "Is this *domestic* cheese?" The woman made her repeat the question three or four times to be sure she was hearing correctly. Nobody has any idea where she heard the term—sure pulled that mom up short. If she was an Alpha Mom, it prolly pushed her close to her edge, thinking she'd just encountered her first Alpha Toddler.)

Then we have the *Beta* Moms. We are the ones that the Alpha Moms trust only to bring the paper towels and trash bags to the parties. Beta Moms show up late, running down the halls, flip-flops flapping on the floor, breathing hard, sweating, hair in a straggly knot, no makeup, scrub pants, and an oversized T-shirt—frantic because we actually forgot this stupid party until we dropped off the car pool and overheard one of the Alpha's kids talking about her mom renting a live parrot for the event and perching him in the banyan tree she made out of grocery sacks and twine. Totally freaked out, we roared off in our old Volvo sedan because the party was due to start in twenty minutes and we were ten minutes away from anyplace that sold paper towels and trash bags, which was our only assignment, and we'd forgotten them. We didn't know it, of course, but we needn't have rushed—actually could have skipped it entirely because, naturally, Alpha Mom has brought extras . . . just in case.

Dads were not mentioned, and that right there seems worthy of research to *me*.

Beta Mom Invents New Game — Then Drinks Daiquiris to Celebrate

Tammy, of the Kansas Tammies, had herself three frying-size kids who had found all of her buttons and were jumping up and down on them repeatedly—on account of they were "bored."

Irritating the crap outta Mom is better than doing *nothing*, I suppose, so they were hard at it. She knew she had to come up with something to distract them or she was going to end up in prison by lunchtime. And she was a Beta Mom, so it had to be fast and labor-free. She was dealing with two boys, ages five and seven, and one girl, age four, so it didn't exactly have to be backgammon. Spying a large jar full of change, she was seized by a brilliant inspiration that rewarded her with a lovely afternoon in the hammock sipping peach daiquiris as she watched her happy children scuttling about the backyard.

She told them she was throwing out ten quarters and they each had to find three—that was the rule—but the luckiest kid would find and keep that last extra quarter! They went wild. It wasn't long before each of them ran to her, breathless, and reported that they had found their three, and the fervent search for that last quarter was on with a vengeance. It lasted all afternoon, in fact, and she never did tell them that she threw out only nine!

Let's Eat!

You can relax now that you know that, yes, there *is* food in this book, too. And let me further relieve your mind by telling you up front that, yes, it's all Sweet Potato Queen–type food: guaranteed to pack on the pounds and jack up your disposition in a most delightful way.

I searched—not far and wide, that would be too Alpha for my lazy-ass Beta self—but maybe close and narrow for a little while—for any hints that I thought might actually be helpful to hungry but harried parents. I thought I'd really happened on a handy source when I picked up a package of ground turkey and it had a little sticker on the label emblazoned with *"Healthy Tip #3—* pre-prepare quick meals for when you're hungry and in a hurry."

After putting all the other groceries away—none of *them* offered me any hints on their labels—I eagerly ripped off the tiny pamphlet, anxious to see what invaluable tip they might offer that I could in turn share with y'all.

I swear to you—all it said was that if you cooked stuff ahead of time, you could "dodge the diet downfall" and keep your daily caloric intake to a minimum—which is, they say, a Good Thing. Under "Meal Ideas" on the same paper, here's the Big Idea: Make homemade chili (with their ground turkey, of course) and freeze it in serving-sized containers. Well—DUU-UHHHH. Thank God they *told* us this, I'm thinking, otherwise how would we ever know that it would be so convenient for us to have pre-prepared supper stuff just waiting in the freezer for us to come grab it, thaw it, and feed it to our frantic families?

I found this "hint" to be on par with that great old Steve Martin routine—you know the one, "How to be a millionaire—and not pay *any* income tax." He goes on and on about how he has come up with this *amazing* plan for becoming a million-aire—tax-free! When he finally gets around to actually telling us how to do this for ourselves, he leads with "*First*—get a mil-lion dollars . . ."—like, nothing to it. So—here you go—*first*, cook a whole buncha stuff and put it in the freezer.

They offered no suggestions on, say, how to find the *time* to pre-prepare a big wad of food for future use—when we can't even find time to cook for right this very minute. There were also zero suggested recipes—but they do have a Web site—if you've got time to go hunt around online while your starving family is gnawing on the windowsills and doorknobs, just to keep their jaws in working order in case food is ever presented to them again in this life.

I'm not sure your kids will eat anything in this section—prolly for sure they won't if they're picky. Here's hoping you do *not* have any picky eaters at your house—but if you do, I know you need a little something to perk *you* up, for sure—so I hope you'll find a tasty morsel or two in here to help you out.

Wet Brownies Ice Cream

Might as well start with something that even the picky eaters will eat, I reckon. Never much problem selling dessert.

In my opinion, most commercially prepared chocolate ice creams just miss the mark when it comes to the "chocolate" part of their makeup. I mean, if you're eating something chocolate, one would assume that you had a desire for a reasonably intense chocolaty experience, no? And they are just too wimpy—not enough oooh-yeah in the chocolate department. So, here's some by-god chocolate ice cream for you. It's so very chocolaty, it's almost like a bowl of wet brownies. It's a huge pain in the ass to make—but completely worthwhile, I think.

❖   ❖   ❖

GET 12 EGG YOLKS and mix 'em up with 6 cups whole milk and then stir in 4 cups sugar and cook all that for what seems like *forever*, until it gets thick enough to coat your stirring spoon. (Really, this is endless—have a happy helper assist with the stirring or you'll get bored and quit and it will scorch and you'll have to eat that crappy store-bought not-chocolaty-enough stuff.)

Then remove it from the heat, sift in 1⅓ somewhat generous cups Hershey's cocoa in the brown box, and beat till it's smooth and creamy. Let it cool and then add 8 cups of half-and-half and 4 running-over teaspoons good vanilla. It's really better if this can sit in the fridge overnight—but not a deal breaker if it can't.

Put it in your ice cream freezer and whirl away—it makes a gallon of heaven.

Alpha Mom Stuff in a Pumpkin

The pumpkin aspect of this recipe is, in my opinion, totally optional and I would never in a million years fool with it—because I am a big ole Beta, but if you're a busy little Alpha and want to fritter away an afternoon messing with the stupid pumpkin, fine by me. I got this recipe from my sister-in-law, Bitsy Browne, a world-renowned Alpha, so when I sampled it for the first time, it *was*, in fact, a full-pumpkin affair and it was admittedly pretty cute and I was happy to see it, happy that Bitsy had gone to the trouble—but if you have it at *my* house, it'll be in a bowl.

❖ ❖ ❖

WHILE THE OVEN is preheating to 375°F, wash a big ole punkin'
and then cut the top off of it and hollow it all out. Brush the inside of
it with 2 tablespoons melted butter and ½ teaspoon ground ginger.
Brush the outside of it with salad oil. Put the top on and bake the
whole pumpkin for 30 minutes—this makes it "look pretty," plus
the hot pumpkin will serve as a sort of chafing dish—attractively
keeping the stuffing hot on a buffet table. (Like I *care*.)

Okay, now for the part you can actually *eat*: Brown 2 pounds
ground pork sausage with 1 pound ground round and then
drain it well. Add ½ cup chopped celery and 1 cup chopped
onion and cook until the onion is transparent—then add 4 cups
croutons, 1 cup chopped walnuts, and 1 cup dark brown sugar.
Stir in 2 tablespoons melted butter and 2 tablespoons orange
juice. Put it all in the pumpkin and bake for 30 minutes. Serve
with *Fritos*!

Even Bailey Will Eat This Squash

BOIL 3 OR 4 POUNDS of yellow squash or zucchini with 1
chopped onion until tender. Then drain it and mash it all up
with a potato masher, dump in 1 or 2 cups shredded sharp
Cheddar, and fold in 2 beaten egg whites. Put it all in a
greased casserole dish and top with crushed saltines—maybe

pour a little bit of melted butter on there if you like—and bake it at 350°F until it bubbles around the edges. Presto—your kid is now a squash eater.

Carrots a Kid Could Love

PEEL ABOUT a dozen carrots and split 'em in half lengthwise. Boil in lightly salted water until they get tender but not mushy. Drain them well. Then melt a half stick of butter (or 4 tablespoons Benecol-type stuff) in a heavy skillet, adding 1 to 2 tablespoons lemon juice and 2 tablespoons dark brown sugar (I use the brown Splenda—love it) and cook it, stirring until it thickens. Put the drained carrots in there and stir 'em around until they're all well glazed with the goo and heated through.

Beta Moms' Fabulous Beanie Sammiches

*B*eta Moms lie down to nap and dream of running off with the guy who invented the Crock-Pot. If ever there was a more *Beta* device, I don't know about it—and I need to know—bad. I do love me a Crock-Pot. You can mix this stuff up the night before—it's a one-pot dump and that's all—and turn it on when you leave in the morning or when you go back to bed in the morning—whatever, they don't care, they'll cook up fine no matter what you're doing. These are also fairly low cal/low fat—not that I give a rip.

❖ ❖ ❖

IN THE BELLY of your big-ass Crock-Pot, put 10 or 12 boneless, skinless chicken thighs. (Don't worry if you've got a picky eater who will *only eat white meat*—it's gonna be in shreds and they won't be able to determine the color—just tell 'em whatever makes 'em happy and move on.) Add 4 big cans of baked beans (I use Bush's), 3 cups chopped onion, 2 cups bottled barbecue sauce (I use McClard's [www.mcclards.com] because it doesn't have high-fructose corn syrup), 2 tablespoons yellow mustard (French's, for sure), and 2 teaspoons each chili powder, sugar (I use Splenda because I'm an addict), and salt. Cover and cook on high for 5 to 6 hours or on low for 8 to 12 hours. Take the chicken out, shred it, and put it back in. Depending on how much liquid was released by the chicken, sometimes it's a little too "soupy." If yours appears to be watery, just dump it all into a big pot and cook it for a few minutes on the stove over medium heat, uncovered, until it cooks down enough to suit you—no trouble at all. Be sure you stir it often—it'll stick if you're not careful. Serve on split hamburger buns—but you'll have to eat it with a fork unless you eat it in an empty wading pool or something—*reeeal* messy. (If you have only a small Crock-Pot, cut all the ingredients in half.)

Royal Trail Mix

▪▪▪▪▪▪▪▪▪▪▪▪▪▪▪▪▪▪▪▪▪▪▪▪

A Queen, dear to my heart always, but alas, anonymous, gave me this yumbo stuff while I was out on my last book tour. She did not write her *name* on the recipe, and so when I bless her in my prayers, which I shall do every night for the rest of my *life,* I can refer to her only as That Fabulous Woman Who Gave Me That Great Stuff with the Cranberries in It. Hopefully, she will see this and make herself known to me.

❖ ❖ ❖

PREHEAT YOUR OVEN to 250°F and while that's warming up, grease a 13 by 9 by 2-inch glass baking dish and spread 3½ cups pecan halves in an even, mostly single layer in the bottom of it. In a glass bowl, mix ¼ cup brown sugar (she says use *light*—y'all know how I feel about that stuff, but we should trust her this one time) and ¼ cup light corn syrup, and microwave it on *high* for 1 minute, then stir it and zap it again for 30 seconds to 1 minute more—until it's boiling merrily. Then take it out, stir it, and add 1 running-over (my suggestion as always) teaspoon vanilla and ¼ teaspoon baking soda, again stirring until well blended.

Drizzle that stuff over the pecans, smear it around with a wooden spoon until it's evenly distributed, and bake it for 1 hour—stirring every 20 minutes with the wooden spoon. Cover a big cookie sheet with foil, and when the pecans come out of the oven, dump 'em onto the cookie sheet and spread 'em out evenly with a greased spatula. Let that cool completely, and then kinda bust it up with a wooden spoon and dump it in a big bowl and mix it with 1½ cups dried cranberries and a half cup or so of shredded coconut (more or less, depending on how much you love coconut).

She says it will keep for a couple of weeks in an airtight container—and that is prolly true as long as nobody TASTES it during that time. I can assure you, if somebody gets a BITE of it, it won't last more than an hour after that.

Fried Noodles

▪▪▪▪▪▪▪▪▪▪▪▪▪▪▪▪▪▪▪▪▪▪▪▪▪▪▪▪▪▪

Yet another yumbo concoction that someone gave me *without their name* attached. God bless her, too. There is no discernible nutritional value to these that I can tell—but they are *excellent* for the disposition.

❖ ❖ ❖

YOU JUST BOIL some extra-wide egg noodles and drain them. Then you melt enough butter in a skillet to cover the bottom of the pan and dump the noodles in there, kinda mash 'em down, and fry 'em in the butter—flipping them over as needed—until they get golden brown and crispy. (Do not *hesitate* to add more butter at any time, should you detect the slightest shortage.) You can put whatever spice on them you like—I'm partial to crushed red pepper in small doses. Of course, you can't use that if you're giving it to kids, they'll have conniptions (kin to hissies) — but you could use kosher salt and they'd lap it up. So, if you don't feel inclined to share on a particular evening, bring on the red pepper!

Sneaky Treats

▬▬▬▬▬▬▬▬▬▬▬▬▬▬▬▬

There's *fruit* in these, but if you don't tell 'em, they won't know — when these are cooked, it's weird, you can't really tell what's in 'em. So keep your mouth shut and they'll eat the fruit. Of course, it's coupled with *white bread*, so you've prolly traded a positive for a negative, but hey — they've just invented that new white bread that's supposedly Not Poison, so maybe try that to soothe your Alpha Mom conscience. Betas don't have one so we don't care.

❖ ❖ ❖

PREHEAT THE OVEN to 350°F. Mix together 1 teaspoon vanilla, 1 8-ounce package softened cream cheese (can be light), and ½ cup well-drained crushed pineapple. Separately, mix together 1 cup sugar (Splenda!) and 2 teaspoons cinnamon. Decrust 18 slices of the white bread of your choice and spread your pineapple stuff on each slice, then fold the two sides to the middle and brush them with ¼ cup melted butter. Roll 'em in the cinnamon/sugar mix and bake 'em for about 20 minutes. *You will die,* these are so good.

Queen Chris and Bob-Daddy's Melted Salad

▟▛▟▛▟▛▟▛▟▛▟▛▟▛▟▛▟▛▟▛▟▛

Okay, it's spinach dip—but if you tell your kids it's "melted salad," they'll at least try it, and I say spinach is good for them, no matter what you have to do to it to get them to eat it.

❖ ❖ ❖

PREHEAT THE OVEN to 350°F. Thaw a 10-ounce package of frozen chopped spinach and squeeze it as dry as you can. Mix it with 2 8-ounce packages softened cream cheese, 2 cups shredded Monterey Jack, 1 cup grated Parmesan, 1 small finely chopped onion, 1 14-ounce can drained chopped artichoke hearts, 2 10-ounce cans Ro-tel tomatoes and green chilies, 2 teaspoons ground cumin, 2 teaspoons chili powder, and 1 teaspoon garlic powder. Put it all in a 2½-quart (that's more than a half gallon—yaaaay!) dish and bake it, uncovered, for 30 minutes or until bubbly. Of course, it's excellent on *Fritos*!

Yes, It's One More Dump Cake Variation

▟▛▟▛▟▛▟▛▟▛▟▛▟▛▟▛▟▛▟▛▟▛

Queen Penny of Centennial, Colorado, brought me this dee-light in a baking dish when I was in Denver at that glorious bookstore The Tattered Cover. She calls it "Apple Crack," and one bite will tell you why—you just gotta have more and more and *more* and there's never enough of it to satisfy you. I think it's the more-than-usual amount of butter and the pecans that make the difference here—you be the judge.

❖ ❖ ❖

PREHEAT THE OVEN to 325°F. Spray the ubiquitous 9 by 13 by 2-inch pan with Pam. Spread 2 cans of apple pie filling evenly in the bottom. Mix together 2 *sticks* melted butter with 1 box yellow cake mix, 1 cup dark brown sugar, and 1 teaspoon cinnamon to make a thick paste. Spread that evenly over the pie filling and top with 2 cups chopped pecans. Bake for 40 to 45 minutes until crispy and brown on top. I think this may be *The* Ultimate Dump Cake—but perhaps by the next book, one of y'all will have brought me yet another variation. Here's hoping!

Tammy Georgia's 80-Proof Cherry Pie

Obviously, this one is Special and Just for Mommies—maybe the occasional daddy if he's good—but definitely *not* for the kiddos. Tammy Georgia invented this when she and her friends were all struggling to survive their daughters' teen years. T-Georgia said her mantra for those years was "She'll be a lovely adult. She'll be a lovely adult." And those words, coupled with her 80-proof cherry pie, got her and all her buddies through that very rough parenting patch known as adolescence.

❖ ❖ ❖

THIS ONE IS perfect for all of us Betas who cannot/will not make piecrust. All you need is one glass and these two ingredients: Zubrowka Bison Grass vodka and apple juice. Tammy sent me the vodka and I have tried this, so I can absolutely vouch for its taste and efficacy. When you mix together 1 part Zubrowka and 2 parts apple juice, what it *tastes* like is a nice cool drink of cherry pie, and what it *feels* like is any martini you have ever had. Take two and call me in the morning.

Naps and Other Sleeping Opportunities

I n my opinion, one of the very best features of your new baby is its built-in requirement for massive amounts of sleep. You will want to see to it that that requirement is met and/or exceeded at *all* times. Hell exacts an incredibly steep price tag when this requirement is ignored—and though you, Mom, will bear the brunt of this penalty, pretty much everybody within earshot of your baby will help pay that price. Hear me and heed my words: **NAP TIME IS SACRED.** It is to be honored and adhered to above all things. *Nothing* else in this *life* will *ever* rival your baby's nap time in importance. A sleeping baby is just about *the* most swell thing you will ever encounter in your whole entire life. That baby needs to nap—and *you need to be right alongside there,* napping yourownself.

There is nothing you need to do, nowhere you need to be,

nobody you need to see, that's worth missing y'all's nap. Screw the laundry, damn the dishes, the hell with housekeeping of any kind—put that baby down for a nap and you go down, too. I'm talking morning *and* afternoon. Get your ass in there and sleep. Your body has just performed the most monumental task in the universe—manufacturing another human being—and it is plumb tuckered out from the procedure. If you're breast-feeding, you are personally creating, on-site, the sole suste-nance of that new human, and you're the primary delivery system as well. This will wear you slap out.

Your baby is growing exponentially at every moment—you can almost watch them do it—and the flood of new stimuli and experiences is overwhelming for that brand-new little brain. The baby *needs* to nap, and sometimes you have to insist and be willing to enforce that insistence. That can mean holding, rock-ing, or lying beside a yowling infant for an hour before victory can be claimed—but, believe me, if you are unyielding in your determination, that baby *will* nap.

And as I said, you need to nap, too. The world will be a much better place for you and those around you if you and that baby grab a few z's. I cannot tell you how many severely fraz-zled mothers I have encountered who look at me with those hollow, haunted, I'm-in-hell eyes and say that little Jimbo or baby Sally "doesn't" or "won't" nap. I'm telling you, there has never been a baby born who won't nap if somebody will take the time and put in the effort to see that it happens.

This does mean that on some days, you may not get all your phone calls made. You may not get the errands run. You may not even get a *shower* until after ten p.m. — but none of that matters if you get that baby to take a morning and an afternoon nap. It will totally not matter if you also take those naps — because you won't be so tired you can hardly inflate your lungs.

I feel so sorry when I'm at the grocery store or, even worse, at the *mall* to see some poor little person just bawling its heart out — obviously worn out and about an hour past nap time — while Mama is just shopping away, so accustomed to her child's tired crying, it no longer bothers her. Crying baby is a permanent part of her background noise.

I don't care if Sean Connery is signing thighs and giving away free Fendi bags — if it's nap time, you need to plan on catching Sean next time he's in town. Again I say, nap time is sacred — and it shares that holiest-of-holies billing with bedtime.

And don't be wagging that baby out at night past bedtime. If there is something going on that you think you just *cannot* miss or you will surely die (like that Sean Connery thigh/Fendi bag thing), then you find *somebody* to hang out at your house and put that baby to bed for you while you horse around with Sean.

This is one of those things you need to think about *before* you start a family: *Your life is over.* It's about somebody else now for quite a number of years. Suck it up. You *did* know the job was dangerous when you took it.

And while I'm on a rant here, let me just tell you what I

think about all those so-called "experts" in child rearing who tell you to put your baby in a dark room by itself and let it scream itself to sleep—in the name of "learning to calm itself." Here's what I think: I think they are totally full of shit and they are the meanest assholes ever to draw breath.

What your baby "learns" from this is that *you* cannot be trusted. What other possible message is there for somebody who cannot take care of themselves? If you are a baby, by definition, you are totally dependent on somebody else to do everything for you. The only thing you get here with is your ability to cry, and when you use that one tool, *most* of the time, your need gets met. Somebody bigger than you will show up and eventually figure out just what it is that you're crying for or about and fix it, and then all is right with your world once more. Then, all of a sudden, the sun goes down and all the big people punch out. Where the hell are they? You're screaming your head off and nada—you get nothing. You don't even remember what it was you were wanting or needing—now you're just hollering because you're completely freaked out that you're apparently all alone in the world. And you cry until sleep overcomes you and you just pass out from sheer exhaustion.

Let me ask you something. Is there a time that lives in your memory—from childhood to adult—doesn't matter—can you ever *recall* a time when you were all alone and you cried yourself to sleep? Did that feel like a positive learning experience to you?

Another question: Have you ever read in any self-help

book or column—have you ever heard even the ubiquitous Dr. Phil suggest—that, for a person of any age, from grammar school to the nursing home, a good way to deal with anxiety or depression or to overcome any fear of any kind would be to put that person in a dark room by themselves and let them just scream it out?

I know *full-grown* people who cannot be alone for five minutes in the *daytime*. I know forty-year-old women who won't spend the night alone in their homes if their husbands go out of town. I've seen plenty of adults who are scared of the dark. The advantage that *these* people have is that they can use their phone to call somebody if they're lonely or afraid. They can have a friend come sleep over or they can get in their cars and drive to their mama's house for the night. They can leave every light in the house on all freaking night long if they want to, and other grown-up people will support them in all this and tell them that is *just fine*, if that's what they need to do to feel safe. Plus sufferers are encouraged, exhorted even, to seek regular therapeutic assistance. *Nobody* is *ever* told to just gut it out—a few nights of screaming and you'll be fine, really.

But poor little babies. Those self-help gurus all pretty much follow the same doctrine when it comes to the *one segment* of the population that really *can't* do anything for themselves about their fears and anxieties: Let 'em scream, it helps them mature. (It also makes for a pretty solid client base for the therapists down the road, I'm thinking.)

We're always trying to force behaviors on little kids that we don't ascribe to ourownselves. Like sharing. When you're little, people are always on your ass to *share* this and *share* that, and they get all bent outta shape when you don't immediately embrace the idea. And what does *everybody* do at the very earliest opportunity? Of course, we get our *own stuff*. When the very cute and precocious Addison was about three years old, her folks began construction on a new house in which she, Addison, was promised *a room of her very own*. Well, time dragged on and the contractors turned out to be less than honest, and by the time the lawsuits were settled and the house was finished, Addison was five, and her patience had run completely out at around three and a half. It had been such a very looooong two years for Addie's parents—between the piece-of-crap builder, the slew of lawyers required to rid them of the piece-of-crap builder, the building itself—all to the tune of the constant high-pitched whine of their little girl, who *really could not wait* for her *own room.*

I imagine that moving day was the best day those folks will ever have in this life. *Finally* Addison would *shut up* about the freakin' *room,* already. And, sure enough, as soon as they walked through the doorway to spend their very first night in the new house that included Addison's own personal room, she took off for it and stayed in there, happy as a pig in the sunshine, nary a peep out of her after the initial "yippee" as she entered.

The parents busied themselves with unpacking and arranging and generally basking in the new house glow, and by and by, they dropped by ole Addie's room to see how she was enjoying her new solo space. Oh, she was enjoying it *just fine*, thankyouverymuch. She was also enjoying that brand-new set of *Sharpies* with which she had indelibly written on every wall, door, baseboard, windowsill, and piece of furniture—in big black kindergarten letters— *"My Room."*

I think they decided to leave it until she left for college.

Brother's Keeper. Low Pay, Few Benefits

S ome children absolutely delight in the arrival of tiny new
siblings in the nest—none that I know of personally, mind
you, but I've heard of it happening. I think. I don't know,
maybe I dreamed it or just made it up. It didn't happen at *my*
house, for instance. For me, it was my big seester, Judy—who
was none too happy about *my* arrival only a few months after
her sixth birthday. For seventy-five magical months, she had
been It—the only apple in the family's eyes. Then, without her
prior approval and surely just to spite her, I was not only begot-
ten and born but brought home to beleaguer her bliss. And you
know how it is when they bring home a new baby—they never
take it *back*—it is just *there,* day in, day out, all the time.

People come to *see* The Baby, they *talk* about The Baby,
they want to *hold* The Baby, they even bring *gifts* for The Baby.

And it never gets any better. Pretty soon The Baby starts to laugh and make stupid baby noises and everybody goes wild. The Baby learns to crawl and you'd think it discovered penicillin. Actual upright steps taken by The Baby—the first human to tread on Mars could not be more heralded. *Words* from The Baby—you would think they came from a Burning Bush. Geez.

I can understand the older child's misery at feeling displaced in the family spotlight, but Judy's reaction to my arrival and subsequent permanent status in the home has always been a mystery to me since none of that stuff happened around me that I could tell.

Literally, these are the *only* stories that have ever been shared with me regarding my own infancy:

1. I was terrified of everything and everyone from the moment they brought me home from the hospital.
2. When I learned to crawl, I ate ant poison at a neighbor's house and had to have my stomach pumped.
3. In all of my baby pictures I am frowning—I didn't smile for a camera until I was probably seven years old.

That's it—that is My Life before I had memory or words as shared with me by my family. I have no idea what my first word was, when I learned to walk, what made me laugh.

But it would appear that whatever attention I did manage to garner was more than Judy could spare—Judy's life was in shambles and there was no relief in sight for her. And so of course, as soon as I could identify faces, I loved hers. Lucky Judy. From the moment I could move about on my own, I wanted only to take myself wherever she was. Whither she goest, I would go. I would sleep where she slept, eat what she ate. Her people would be my people; her God, my God. I worshipped and adored her. She was the perfect person in my eyes. I wanted only to be in her presence my every waking moment.

To Judy, I was breathing the air formerly reserved especially for her. I was a leech. I was dog doo on her Sunday shoes. She despised me.

Ain't it funny how two people can be in the same family, at the same time, and experience the whole thing in such completely different ways? I grew up thinking how lucky was I to have the *best* big sister in the whole wide world—and she grew up thinking life sucked after six.

The Cutest Boy in the World, my husband, Kyle, assures me that his sister Cindy is still pissed off that they brought him home that hateful, fateful day forty-five years ago.

Queen Cheri said her three-year-old son was less than thrilled with the new baby sister she brought home for him and asked if she wouldn't please "return her to Wal-Mart, I think she's broke—she won't do anything but cry—try getting another *boy.*"

I guess we often expect that little girls will have more "natural" instinct and desire to take care of babies, but Crystal's daughter Megan totally debunked that theory. The child never cared for babies or even baby dolls—not the least bit interested in either. When she was about seven, the "hot" toy that Christmas was a baby doll with all manner of "ailments" that the little mama could "make all better." Little Megan, dry and sarcastic from the womb, watched the ad on TV, looked at Crystal, and, completely deadpan, said, "Mom, you buy that thing for me and I will just let it die."

For some reason, Crystal thought it might change Megan's attitude if she was to help with the babies in the nursery at church. Megan grudgingly agreed to participate in this boondoggle. She walked into the nursery, and as soon as she sat down, somebody handed her a baby—which she greeted with a resigned sigh and rolled-up eyes. Later, Crystal asked her what she had expected—since it *was*, after all, the nursery. Megan said, "Well, I didn't think they would hand me a little drooling alien!" Crystal is not expecting grandchildren—ever.

Katelyn, ten, turned her ankle a few weeks before Christmas, and no star of the silver screen ever delivered a more dramatic portrayal of unbearable agony. Beta Mom Debbie decided to take her in and have it X-rayed even though the "Mother of the Year" contest was long since over and Deb did not even place—or care. Brother Nick, seven, had no choice but to go along for the ride to the ER and wait for the verdict. He clearly had Something on His Mind about this little excursion, and it did not occur to anyone that this could have been a deep concern for the welfare of his big sister and her ankle. If that had occurred to anyone, it would have been a complete mistake—Nick was, as usual, thinking about Nick.

> NICK: Mom, how much does an X-ray COST?
> MOM: I'm not sure, Nick—we'll find out soon.
> NICK: Does it cost a hundred dollars?
> MOM: I'm not sure, hun, but insurance will pay for most of it.
> NICK: Will it cost fifty dollars?
> MOM: I honestly don't know, Nick.
> NICK (to his poor injured sister Katelyn): If this is more than a hundred dollars, it will come out of *your* Christmas, not *mine*. Isn't that right, Mom?

Both Mom and Katelyn were rendered speechless by Nick's thoughtful query—Mom from hysterical laughing, Katelyn from sisterly fury. No broken bones were revealed on the X-ray, and, amazingly, none were incurred in the waiting room either.

If this is not your first child, you might be misguidedly tempted to try to assuage the angst your other children may be experiencing in their less-than-enthusiastic reactions to the upcoming addition to the family. You might even go so far as to enlist the aid of the disgruntled party(s) in the naming of the new child. This does not bode well for the newcomer. Denise made this mistake. When her son Michael was five and a half, Denise brought home sister Darby. When he was eight, he was informed that there would be yet another little bundle coming home by and by. He did not receive this as glad tidings of great joy—to the contrary, he advised his parents that Darby had ruined his life and he simply could not take any more of "their" kids.

Feeling at least a particle of the guilt Michael had hoped to inflict upon them, Denise and her husband racked their brains to try think of ways to "make it easier" for "poor" Michael, to make him feel "more included" and whatnot. They decided to award little Michael the extraordinary privilege of selecting his new little brother's middle name—telling him that the child's first name would be "Sawyer."

Michael spent the next few days deep in thought over this awesome prerogative and its attendant responsibility. Finally, he said that he had decided he really, really would like for the baby's middle name to be "Peter." They were so impressed by the time and care he had devoted to his selection—and that he didn't pick the name of any friend or family member—nor was it the name of any cartoon character or superhero. It really appeared at first blush that Michael had warmed to the idea of a new brother. Then they said the two names together and the jig was, as they say, up.

Penii

When you become pregnant, there is a pretty good chance that one day you will be going home from the hospital—having given birth to a baby with a penis. Although, truth be told, for much of the child's life (and nearly all of the subsequent man's), it will, at times, seem that you have given birth to a penis with a very small boy attached.

There is absolutely nothing in this world—nor in any worlds that may lie out yonder—that holds for him any comparable level of fascination—the word "delight" would not be too strong here—to that which he feels for his own penis. It is truly the center of his universe, and virtually any decision he makes in life can somehow be reduced to "happy penis/sad penis." There are *no* degrees of separation betwixt him, his penis, and the world at large. He has more names for it than he does for love or for anything or anybody for whom he feels love. It is the one companion whose company never bores him. There is no transgression for which he cannot forgive his penis—his penis can do no wrong.

His penis is endlessly entertaining and he never fails to feel somewhat excited by the sight of it, the thought of it, and/or the feel of it. It is captivating to him in all phases of its development. He gazes with admiration upon its turgidity and with loving affection when, spent, it lies resting peacefully. He finds that nothing can soothe the savage beast within him quite so completely as a little one-on-one time with his penis.

He loves it by the dawn's early light, in the noonday heat, at teatime, and in the dusky dusk. He loves it like the muskrat loves its musk. He loves it at sunrise and sunset and for all the sunrises and sunsets of his entire life. He loves it by starlight, moonlight, candlelight, and flashlight. He loves it in the pitch-black dark and in the even darker hour just before dawn. If he could pick only one thing in the universe to be stranded with him on a desert island, his penis would be chosen and there would be no close second. Same for being stuck in an elevator, trapped in a coal mine, or buried alive.

He loves it in a box. He loves it with a ... oh, never mind— you get the idea without the necessity of putting the visual of animals in there. He loves it with any rhyme you can think of and he loves it in free verse. He loves it a whole encyclopedia-worth.

He loves to think about it, look at it, touch it, touch it, touch it, touch it, touch it, and then touch it some more. He loves to talk about it and he also *really* loves for Others to engage in all of the above. If he could hold weekly—daily? hourly?—seminars featuring nothing but his own penis and have people come from all points of the compass to gaze in wonder at it, hold group discussions about it, and then have some afternoon sessions of "hands-on" experiential sessions with it—well, this would give us all an opportunity to witness the glory of an artist consumed with passion for his work.

He might draw a very thin line at having it actually worshipped—might. If he could bring himself to draw such a line, with much faux-protesting that, after all, "It's *just* a penis—albeit *mine*," he would no doubt be secretly pleased if people did it anyway.

Waggling it—whether at his own reflection in the mirror, at one willing or unwilling (it matters not) spectator in the privacy of a personal residence or hotel room, or at hundreds (again willing or un—makes no difference) at a drunken frat party or poolside on a crowded cruise ship—waggling is *always* hilarious—to him.

He gets nearly as many belly laughs from hiding it by tucking it and its accoutrements between his legs—only to jump astride, allowing everything to spring back to its rightful place—in a bizarre version of peekaboo.

He loves its every function—a lot. A lotta lot. Whooooboy-hidee—does he ever. I mean, a baby boy loves lots of his other body parts, too, from the very beginning—you know, how they find their thumbs first and they point at everything with their thumbs and they put their thumbs on and in everything they can reach and that is just sooooo much fun for 'em. But once they find the whole hand and then those little hands find that penis—well, it's all over for the thumbs and hands. From that day forward, it is *alllll* about the pee-pee.

I guess the discovery of the Hard-on is probably the Best Day of the Boy's Life, forever and ever, amen. It's all downhill for them from that point—nothing else they experience or en-counter will *ever* live up to *that*—except, of course, for the next time he has one. It never loses its magic, but when you're only three you can get away with a whole lot more than you can later in life. You can talk about what's in your pants in great detail, with utter abandon, and everybody will just think it's cute.

When Queen Pam was driving down a busy Nashville street one afternoon, her two young sons, Robby and John, lashed into their car seats, occasional rearview glances showed her that Robby was drifting off to sleep while John was staring intently out the window. A sudden flurry of movement in the backseat drew her gaze back to the mirror, and she saw John's hands fly up in the air as if he'd just been given the "stick-'em-up" command in an old cops-and-robbers movie, and he let out an ecstatic whoop and announced, *"My penis is getting big and I haven't even touched it!"* Whoo-hoo! Good day for ole John-boy!

One guy I've seen still manages to get away with talking

publicly about his package—but only because he has held on to a major portion of his cute allotment. Late-night talk-show host Jimmy Kimmel (of erstwhile *Man Show* fame; I did love that show—typical guy shit, hilarious)—who I do think is one of the Cutest Boys in the World—occasionally plays a little "man on the street" type game—only, in this case, of course, it is "really cute girl on the street." The game is called Guess What's in My Pants! and he gets really cute girls to feel around on the front of his pants in an effort to determine what he's got in there. He does an hilarious running commentary during their groping, and, to his credit, he really *does* put something in his pants—a can of spray paint, a toy soldier, a half-eaten jelly doughnut—anything goes. I know *plenty* who wouldn't put a thing in there—I'm sure you do as well.

They do make 'em seem like pretty much fun, don't they? What woman doesn't get the concept of penis envy? I mean, once we figure out the deal with them, and they are confusing, are they not? They are so *different* from anything *we* have. Doris recalled that the first time she saw her baby brother's tiny Unit, she thought he had two noses. (She was to learn that later in life, like noses, penises often get stuck in other people's business where they don't belong.) Little Tater Tot Brooke was really pissed off about her own potty-training experience when she observed that her older brother Blake could actually pee on the trees themselves—and did not have to be satisfied with merely watering their roots. Have we not all shared her angst?

Yes, however, I do know of one little two-year-old girl in glittery pink and white cowgirl boots who was seen to be angst-free when she was denied emergency access to the restroom where her mama *formerly* did her banking. Even cowgirls gots to pee, but the surly head teller was less than sympathetic, turning a deaf ear to the plea and a blind eye to the frantic pee dance being done in the bank lobby. Finally, further holding became impossible, but somehow, with the aim of a sharpshooter, our little Annie Oakley managed to very delicately and with the utmost precision direct that stream straight down her leg and into one of her glittery pink and white cowgirl boots. Mama, having completed her bank business, and soggy-boot girl having . . . ahh . . . done *her* business, they squished out, vowing in the future to take their business — all of it — *elsewhere*.

I saw the most BRILLIANT short film on the Sundance Channel once. It was called *Hung*, and it's about a group of lesbians who were somehow granted penii for a day. They woke up one morning and every single one of 'em had a dick. It was hilarious.

It was absolutely sidesplitting to watch the choices each of them made about how to spend their Dick Time. One of them went straight to a Home Depot. One of them went to the beach and tried to pick up women. One of them did nothing but drink gallons of water all day long and stand around outside, peeing on stuff — writing her name, aiming at various and sundry targets of greater and lesser levels of difficulty, and just generally reveling in her ability to whip it out and pee — anywhere, any-time. It must be said that while the pee games were right up at the very top of the barrel-o'-monkeys scale, that glee was nearly eclipsed by the never-ending wonder at the ease and thrill of the whole Whip-Out process.

A couple of them were conspicuously absent for most of the screen time. Of course, the two of them had stayed in bed to-gether for the entire duration of the spell and were half-dead by the time it was over. And then, don't you just *know*, at some point the *rulers* came out. Oh, yeah, even these supposedly highly evolved women — when it came right down to it — they just couldn't resist it — just had to know — even though they had 'em for only twelve hours — they proved one of the most ancient axioms of humankind: Size does matter.

I bet if you could offer 1,000 men their choice of any wish — brilliant mind, big sack of money, ability to leap tall buildings in a single bound — just about anything they could think of — *or* a bigger dick — 999 of 'em would opt for the dick and the other one already *had* a whopper to start with.

My daddy was in the insurance business, and early in his career he actually sold policies, which meant he spent many dinnertimes at the tables of his clients. One evening at just such a dinner, there was a momentary lull in the adult conversation, which was seized by the youngest diner — a small boy about four — who had just been *dying* to reveal what he had learned on his walk in the woods with his gran'paw that day — a blissful afternoon that included, of course, outside peeing. He stood on his chair, throwing his arms out fairly wide, and advised the company with a happy bellow, *"Granddaddy's thang is that long — and brown!"* It must be said that Granddaddy was not as displeased with this announcement as he should have been.

Mealtime discussions of such things are hardly rare. Children are anxious to participate in conversation with adults, and their favorite topic is usually Whatever Is on Their Minds at That Very Second—with very little filtering and/or editing as to content. Queen Karen bore witness to that when her nephew Travis inquired of a male dinner guest if the guest had a penis. The guest allowed, with a snicker, as how he supposed he did. Now, Travis was *trying* to engage the man in a serious discussion and he did not at all appreciate being snickered at. He gave the man a disdainful—even doubtful—look and followed up with, "Well, is it as big as my daddy's?" (Karen did not share with me if any table-side comparisons were conducted at that time, but we can only imagine that the question lingered on everyone's mind. I still wonder to this very day.)

My nephew Trevor Palmer owns the inimitable F & M Patio Bar in New Orleans—everybody who's anybody in N.O. has spent some time on those bar stools, in that photo booth, and/or dancing on that leopard-print pool table. There is a regular crew of happy hour guys who come in every day to sit at the bar and play their own favorite drinking game, which they obviously made up theirveryownselves. Between yammering about what all irritated them in their own personal lives that day and watching an hour or so of what is nearly always Bad News on the TV, they have come up with what seems to me to be a surefire stress reliever—it's quaintly and aptly called "Sucking My Dick" and it goes like this: Say, one guy's employer—we'll call him "John Doe"—really pissed him off that day. He holds them spellbound with the details of John Doe, the bosshole from hell, and as he winds it up, the group will lift their frosty beer mugs on cue and shout with him, *"Here's to John Doe—sucking my dick!!"* And they all just laugh and laugh, and then the next guy has his turn to spew venom about whoever upped his dander that day—it could be just about anybody on the planet, but frequent stars are, of course, ex-wives, cable-company employees, any other person driving on the road at the same time, and all politicians—and they all "toast" that one as well, and so they while away the happy hour in true guy-fashion. Sigh. I must admit, we girls really don't have a satisfactorily zippy substitute for that particular excoriation, and on occasion I do regret that—that and writing our names in the snow are two of life's pleasures just not afforded to us, I reckon.

Never having birthed no boy babies myself, I never endured the difficulty of looking up just in time to witness my three-year-old son shaking off after having successfully completed a satisfying whiz in one of the display toilets at Sears. Nor did I ever find myself strolling across a crowded parking lot, holding the hand of my little boy and wondering why cars were stopping so the people in them could laugh uproariously without running into other cars — and, after checking to make sure my skirt wasn't hiked up over my butt, glancing down to see the cause of all the hilarity: the little boy's hand that was NOT in the hand of his mother was employed in steadily aiming the spumescent stream of urine with which he was spraying weeds, gravel, various forms of litter, and the tires of cars, parked and otherwise. I imagine the intent look of concentration in his darling eyes, little tongue held firmly between his sweet baby lips, the almost smug swagger in his little step that is echoed in his air of satisfied accomplishment as each target is liberally splashed. A small man on a mission — and that mission, in his opinion, a rousing success.

No, I was spared those particular Motherly Moments — not having produced any penis-bearing offspring.

Pint-size Penis People practically all prefer to be perfectly naked most of the time. (I was into the alliteration there but could not think of a *P* word that means "bare-assed," sorry.) Little boys just do seem to love to get naked — and I've not met too many — hmmm — make that *any* — who ever get over it. (The big boys are just about as happy to be nekkid by themselves as they are if and when we get nekkid with them.)

Many moms of boys have told me about their progeny's stellar performances at show-and-tell in kindergarten, and I would probably agree that an artfully displayed penis is nearly always more engaging and entertaining to the class than, say,

Mary Jane's American Girl doll for the fifth time in a row. And a clever little boy known as "Bear" made a most felicitous discovery the first day it was warm enough to wear shorts to kindergarten. The sour old teacher he was cursed to have for his first foray into academia did not think it was the same boon to mankind that Bear did when he showed the class that the great thing about wearing shorts to school was that you could just run your hand right up the leg and grab your pee-pee. Prolly why she *was* so sour, don't you reckon?

My good friend Shelli did such a fine job of teaching her two young sons that it was simply "*not* okay to hit" for any reason. She worked and worked with them, teaching them to be in touch with their feelings and to use their words and to look for nonviolent methods of expressing their displeasure to other people. Ummm-hmmm. *So,* these two young Gandhis come home from school one afternoon and the younger one announces his shocking discovery that "The teacher sure doesn't like it when you pull down your pants in class." Oh, my—I just bet she does not like that a-tall. It took a good bit of discussion to ferret out the means by which the youngster had come to glean this salient bit of info—and so early in the school year, too.

It seems that one of his fellow students had really upset him and caused him to feel a violent surge of anger for which he did not, at the moment, have at the ready any *words* that he felt were big and/or strong enough for fully conveying the enormity of his fury to this other person, but even in this superheated moment, he did recollect that, according to his mama, smacking the crap out of his adversary was not on the "approved" list, and so he did the *only* thing he could think of on such short notice, and that was to moon the kid. Many guffaws and high-fives were shared between the two boys, naturally, as Shelli struggled and failed to maintain any momlike decorum. But eventually she was able to speak clearly enough to admonish them that, for future reference, in-class mooning was added to the list of Things You Wouldn't *Think* You Would Have to Tell Them *Not* to Do.

Queen Di added a similar item to her own list when she observed her son and his buddies on the swimming pool slide. No one else appeared to have noticed that at the top of the slide, just before launching themselves poolward, they were surreptitiously ooching down their swimsuits so that during the big downhill swoosh, there was no fabric between their behinds and the slide. Not wishing to call undue attention to this latest manifestation of maleness, she casually strolled over to where they were climbing out before running up the ladder to repeat the performance. From behind her sunglasses and with one of those deadly ear-to-ear *non*-smiles that only mothers can achieve with their facial muscles, she ever so sweetly asked them through clenched teeth just what they thought they were doing. To which they replied, in tones dripping of *"Duuuuhhh,"* from which any person with ears would infer that the asker was a total numbskull, that they went *faster* that way. (And don't you just know that the reason they *knew* this to be true was because their *fathers* had told them so.)

Having only one sister and one daughter, I never found myself, like Queen Angie, faced with the unspeakable dilemma of hearing the soft but panicked whimper of my young son and, upon rushing to his side, discovering that he had somehow managed to get his wee balls stuck in the axle of his toy car. Even though, as a woman and therefore having no balls of her own, this was immediately a source of utter mystery to her, there was clearly no point in trying to discern just exactly *how* this situation came to be—her first and *only* job as the mom was to get them *loose* and pronto—which she did somehow manage to do in that way that moms have of doing the impossible with no information and no tools.

That story gave me pause, though—knowing as we do that They Never Really Grow Up—I wonder if this kind of thing isn't going on in auto-repair shops on a daily basis all over the country? And, if so, who's getting them loose?

Queen Gail found herself facing a similar tragicomedy when she was called upon to render bathtime aid to her six-year-old grandson, Brandon, who had what started out to be a very gratifying relationship with an empty shampoo bottle go sour on him as he learned an important physics lesson about the state of affairs known as a "vacuum." He had plunged his member, willy-nilly—as they are so wont to do their whole *en-*

tire lives—into this handy opening and he had pulled it out, and that seemed good to him so he did it a bunch more times, and by and by his grip sorta clamped down on the bottle and, lo, a mighty suction was born. So much so that it was necessary to cut off the bottom of the bottle in order to free him from his sudsy prison. He wailed, pitiably, "It felt so good at first—but then I couldn't get out of it!" Reckon how many times he'll say *those* words over his lifetime?

Happy with Our Po-pos, Thankyouveramuch

Obviously, if you don't bring home a little penis, you'll more than likely be bringing home a po-po, and, yes, for the most part, you will find that po-pos are much more well behaved than penii. The Cutest Boy in the World, childless but not an igmo (most of the time anyway) has made this very astute observation: If you have a little boy, you only have to worry about ONE dick, whereas if you have a little girl, you have to worry about every dick in the WORLD. (We don't even have to ASK how he figured THAT out. If anyone ever DESERVED to have children, it's this guy.)

I think I speak for all po-po owners when I say that, yeah, the penii do have some convenience features that we lack, but overall we really wouldn't trade—holding, as we do, that major trump card—the ole Multiple Orgasm.

Queen Tammy told me that when her little girl, Bunny, was just so very wee, her favorite pastime was something she called "hanging," during the performance of which Bunny would lie facedown across a chair or ottoman, with her little legs extended out behind her. She would then scissor her legs back and forth for a spell and then get up looking happy. Bunny's clueless father had no, well, CLUE why this activity was so appealing for his precious baby girl, and eventually he voiced his confusion to Tammy, who looked at him like he was THE biggest igmo on the planet and said, "She's MASTURBATING, silly!" Dad was floored—what?—like only little BOYS do it? WHAT an igmo!

Tammy did speak gently to Bunny about the subject of hanging—telling her it was absolutely beyond okay, totally swell, even, to hang—but that it was really more of a private thing. Say, when we're having a sleepover at somebody else's house—we don't hang at their house—we wait till we get home—and Bunny thought that was a good plan—fewer interruptions at home and all. Fine.

One day, after a particularly satisfactory hanging session, Bunny looked up as Tammy came through the room and asked whether or not there were any OTHER ways to hang. Tammy said, well, she didn't know, maybe—and asked if Bunny had TRIED any other ways and Bunny said no, so Tammy said, well, flip over on your back and give it a go. Bunny flipped and flapped her little legs, frowning. Tammy asked how that was.

Bunny allowed as how it was not as good AT ALL—"You don't get the 'tickle part.'" "The tickle part?" Tammy naturally asked. "In your po-po," Bunny patiently replied. "OH!" Tammy said. "Well, that's the best part, isn't it?" Definite affirmative there. Comes under the "If It Ain't Broke" clause.

Potty Training

Performing on the potty is a natural progression for most little people. Kids are incredibly smart and so, fortunately, it really doesn't take much time or expertise for even the dumbest parent to impart this important bit of wisdom to his or her offspring.

Word to the unwise and uninitiated from one who learned oh-so the hard way: When trying to teach a little boy to peepee in the potty, never stand behind him and lean over him—he's liable to pee straight up your nose. (Thanks for the tip, Tara!)

When it came to be Potty Time for Queen Tami and her two-and-a-half-year-old son, Jack, they were heavy into *The Lion King* video, watching it daily and committing to memory every word spoken or sung by Simba, Timon, Pumba, and all those guys. Jack had a firm grasp of the concept of "Hakuna Matata" and the circle of life, but he was not seeing any particular personal benefit to big-boy underpants as opposed to pull-ups.

Queen Tami was well versed in all manner of elementary education, and she was applying every particle of her master's degree in child development to this vexation a-a-a-a-and she was getting *no*-where. Memorial Day weekend rolled around, as it does every year pretty much, but no beach barbecues were on the slate for Tami and Jack. They would be working on a little "home improvement" project. Half of the family was firmly committed to this weekend marking the demise of the diaper at their house—while the other half, it should be noted, was otherwise committed. And so round and round they went, and little or no progress was noted.

Enter Grammy. Good ole pie-baking, cookie-making, grandkid-spoiling, no master's degree Grammy. Well, Grammy showed up with a prize for her favorite grandson—*Lion King* undies. Real big-boy plastic-free underpants—decorated with images of Simba and Timon and Pumba plus a host of little happy-looking bugs. Grammy solemnly presented them to Jack and told him there should be no pooping in these pants or he would have "stinky bugs in his shorts." Brown eyes wide and full of conviction, Jack affirmed, *"No stinky bugs!"*

By and by, Grammy had made her somewhat smug exit, confident that Mom Sense had once again triumphed over Book Sense, and all did, in fact, seem to be progressing positively in the potty department. Tami was puttering in the

120

kitchen, keeping an eye on Jack, who was entertaining himself with minimal supervision in the backyard, which, although surrounded by a chain-link fence, was easily viewable by the steady stream of traffic down the side street.

Jack was within shouting distance but he was not handily snatchable out by the fence where he was presently seen (by many) to have pulled off his Pumba pants and was pooping powerfully into a potted plant. Availing herself of the shouting distance as she galloped out to attempt snatching, Tami hollered, "Jack! What are you doing?" and he gave her, of course, the *obvious* answer, *"No stinky bugs!"*

So, success — I suppose not a complete success . . . but Memorial Day will always have a special distinction for them — and for most of their neighbors.

Little Luke had been a quick study on all aspects of potty usage, but around age four, he began to backslide when it came to cleanup. His mama had to constantly remind him to wash his hands after using the facilities because he was always in such a tearing hurry to get back to playing. On one occasion, she was passing the restroom, heard the toilet flush, but there was no sound of water running before the door flew open and Luke rushed out. She naturally stopped him and ordered him back to the sink, but he protested that he didn't need to wash his hands — on account of he "didn't touch it."

How this was accomplished seemed to Mom to be a mystery worth exploring, and so she escorted him potty-side and requested a demo. He reenacted the scene for her as follows: He would stand right up next to the bowl and stick his belly (and other parts) way out and tinkle. When he was empty, he placed his hands at about belly-button level—and jiggled his tummy—which also caused other parts to shake—thereby enabling him to complete the act with no direct contact with any body parts that would, in his opinion, necessitate the application of soap and water to his hands before exiting the restroom.

Luke's father categorically denies having taught this to his son and we have no definitive proof otherwise, but it does give one pause.

There are and always have been ten gajillion books out there written by "experts" of all kinds claiming to "know" everything there is to know about children—each generation spawns a new body of "knowledge," and I'm sorry, but I've seen parents do everything "right" and end up with Hounds from Hell—and also parents who *are* Hounds from Hell who end up with kids who do everything right. Closely resembles a crapshoot to me—I wish I had more than a bad pun for you here, but really—it's a total crapshoot and I wish us all the best of luck.

Man-oh-man, there is some strange stuff out there about this subject—with all the "expert" advice being pumped out into the universe, it's a wonder we aren't all a whole lot crazier than we are.

In the 1917 tome that my precious darlin' George brought

me, I found a procedure I have never heard of before or since — the author of *The Care and Feeding of Infants* suggested the following bizarre technique for potty training that purported to have a two-month-old child's bowels moving on a regular daily timetable "if training is begun early." *EARLY?* Earlier than two months? Where — in the womb? I swear to you that what I'm about to tell you was actually written down by a grown man, published by another one, *sold* to heaven knows how many blindly trusting women, and perpetrated on no doubt countless helpless babies.

Just to be on the safe side, let me say right here in print in this book with my very own name on the cover that I am passing this information along to you as a *joke*. It was written by a guy more than ninety years ago, and although it is laughable to *read* about such igmonosity, I am quite certain that Child Protection Services would rightly have plenty to say about this, should the method be employed today.

Mothers were instructed to get a small — say, pint-sized — bowl, hold it between their knees, and then sit their little bitty baby's bare behind on that bowl, making sure to prop the little bitty baby's body against their own — since at under two months of age, nobody can sit up by themselves. Moms were supposed to take their little bitty babies through this exercise twice a day — after the morning and afternoon feedings and *always* at the same time — the point being to train the little bitty baby to shit on demand.

The author was aware that the little bitty baby might not fully grasp the point of the exercise immediately, and therefore he suggested that it might be necessary to provide, for the baby's edification, a little "local irritation—as a suggestion of the purpose for which the baby is placed upon the chamber." I shit you not (bad pun number 2—oops, that's number 3) the man then suggested—in print, with his own name on the cover of *that* book—that the new mom could provide this educational stimulus by either "tickling the anus or introducing just inside the rectum a *small cone of oiled paper* or a *piece of soap*" (emphasis added).

He went on to say that in a "surprisingly short time," this part would become unnecessary—simply placing the baby in the position would produce the desired result. I should think so—the mere sight of a pint-sized bowl is probably enough to provide a lifetime of post-traumatic stress disorder. (Come to think of it, it probably accounts for the preponderance of old guys who're always wanting to have their asses tickled with a feather, too.)

The author pointed out how the mother would be spared much trouble and labor—not to mention dirty diapers—by having her baby thusly trained. He failed, however, to offer any projections on the cost of long-term psychotherapy or the everyday wear and tear of living with a seriously disturbed individual.

Speaking of crazy shit (ooooh, bad pun, bad pun), a few

years back, my friend John brought me an actual printed pamphlet that described in detail for us the "art" of defecation.

It was clearly for adult use, having big words like *hemorrhoids* and *constipation* in its text, which sought, more than anything else in life, to promote "rectal health." There was a thought-provoking logo on the front depicting a large intestine wrapped completely around a map of the United States. I imagined all manner of slogans to interpret this striking logo: "The Nation That Goes Together Stays Together"? "There Goes the Country"? "America—We're #1 in #2"? What *were* they thinking?

It is a grand country, after all, where somebody can make what I assume was a good living just by offering *instructions* to grown-up people on ump-making. *Detailed* instructions, mind you. Beginning with what all you need to eat and drink and how often in order to initiate the process whereby your body can create the umps—there are three full steps before you get to the part where he wants you to actually expel them.

I was particularly intrigued by step 5, however, when, having passed the ump, you are instructed, in *no* uncertain terms—quite forcefully, as a matter of fact—to *squeeze the rectum shut.* Hmmmm. I admit I never gave this much—or any—thought before—but the author's unbridled vehemence for step 5 led me to ponder whether or not this had actually been an issue of sufficient scope for the general population to warrant the need for a clearly stated, defined, and delineated step 5 in a training pamphlet.

Okay, fine—it's out there now—if you ever had any doubt at all about what step 5 was supposed to be—mystery solved. Once Elvis leaves the building, *slam the door.*

Mothers of Sons Can Never Retire

SIGH. I hate to be the one to break it to you—but I'm sure it doesn't *really* come as "news" to y'all—that baby boys do one day grow into bigger ones, and, ultimately, great big ones, but "boys" they do always remain, as these tales so aptly demonstrate.

The Cutest Boy in the World and his cousin Danny had both passed "potty training" sometime back and they were, in fact, old enough that they were allowed to go, unsupervised, down to the boat dock at the lake where the two families summered every year. One day shortly after the boys left the house, the parents received a phone call from the dock owner. It was one of those phone calls so typical in the South—they always begin with something like "Y'all ain't gon' believe this shit," and go on to describe what usually is some behavior that is unbelievably bad.

It seems that the two cousins had started off innocently enough, peeing, as young boys are wont to do, in broad daylight on a Saturday afternoon in a public place—off the boat dock. Somehow it devolved into a duel of sorts—literally, a pissing contest, if you will—where they faced each other, peeing on each other's feet and taking progressive backward steps to see who could get the farthest away while still managing to project the stream onto his opponent's feet. This activity has not ever occurred to a girl-type child nor do we believe that it will serve any worthwhile long-term goal for the boy types— but *they* are sure to argue otherwise.

When my daddy was growing up in Attala County, Mississippi—Ethel, to be exact—which is, as I'm sure you know, a *suburb* of Kosciusko—there was no indoor plumbing. This was never of any consequence to my daddy and/or his baby brother, Bub, who would go outside every morning for that most delightful First Pee of the Day, and they would stand side by side and pee on this big sandstone rock.

The rock had many dents and fissures on its surface, but on one side there was a hole that went clear through it—you could see the ground beneath it. On the other side of the rock, there was a hole that went down only a couple of inches. Daddy told Bub that he himself had peed the hole all the way through that rock—and that furthermore, he had *started* that other hole for Bub but Bub was gonna have to pee it the rest of the way through hisownself. And so, every morning, little Bub would stand there, peeing as hard as ever he could into that hole in his unceasing, unflagging efforts to duplicate the peeing prowess of his beloved, much-admired big brother— the liar.

The rock sits by my front door this very day — still with one whole hole and one half-hole. We call it the "Conner Stone." I put it at the front door to *hopefully* discourage — by its location — The Cutest Boy in the World from taking up where Bub left off, but I *do* have my suspicions that The Quest lives on.

You Might Think It's Funny
but It'snot

Babies don't have sinuses, which is really poor planning if you ask me, on account of they do, on occasion, produce a whole big lotta snot. Oh, please—does anybody out there *really* think that the word "mucus" sounds better than "snot"? They both sound pretty pukey to me.

Anyway, babies cannot store snot by sniffing because they have no storage facilities yet. I'm not sure at what age the sinuses develop—I'm sure there's an Alpha Mom out there who can tell us—but knowing that won't help you one bit if you've got a little snot factory cranking away at your house.

They also cannot blow their noses—well, I don't suppose there is any physiological prohibition against it, but rather they don't blow their noses because, frankly, it just doesn't occur to them. (Children don't actually learn to blow their own noses until sometime after puberty, and then only to avoid being called "Snot Face" by the kids on the bus.) Babies are apparently not bothered in the slightest by the rivers of ooogh flowing steadily from their nostrils. Actually, it would seem quite the contrary to anyone exhibiting any intentions toward the *removal* of so much as a dollop of the babies' gross personal product from their faces and surrounding areas—most babies will staunchly resist such efforts and, indeed, put up a fuss of mythic proportions.

They made that snot theirveryownselves and it is adorning theirveryownfaces and garments and living quarters and they just do *not* see where that is *any* business of yours nor why you should concern yourself with it in any way.

Should you be foolish enough to approach this snotty little creature with one of those syringes the how-to books are so keen on—with any thought in your *head* of sticking the end of it up anybody's nose but your *own* and trying to suck up anything with it—well, you will see where Linda Blair got her inspiration for her *Exorcist* performance. Babies' heads *will* rotate 360 degrees, and full-body levitation is not at all unusual before the age of two.

Whoever invented those syringes should be assigned to handle all the requests for putting melted butter up the asses of wildcats—and they should have to use their handy syringes to do the job.

There is nothing more painful to a mother than the illness

of her child—there are no "minor" illnesses when it's your baby. Point of clarification: A sick child causes pain in the heart of the woman who loves that child while a sick *husband* causes a similar level of pain—although in the neck and/or ass—of the woman who is married to that man. Mothers need a well-oiled sense of humor in order to survive family life.

Queen Leigh had been fighting a particularly icky health issue on behalf of her five-year-old daughter, Ashley, and she was not alone—every mother in her kindergarten class was similarly engaged. They just could not seem to get everybody's health bill clean at the same time. Many physicians had written the same prescriptions for this crew numerous times that school year and it was wearing thin for all concerned—well, for the mothers anyway; the kids didn't seem fazed by it.

But one *more* time, Leigh found herself standing in line at the drugstore, waiting for yet another prescription for Ashley, who, always a gregarious child, was having a large time visiting with all the other folks in the queue. An exquisitely dressed, very distinguished-looking older lady came in and took her place at the end of the line, carrying a little boy in her arms. Ashley went right up to them and asked why they were there. The lady replied that she needed to get some medicine for her grandson because he was very sick. Ashley nodded understandingly and commiserated with the woman thusly: "I'm sick, too. I've got head lice." And on and on, in detail that was most painful to her mortified mama, who, as she grabbed Ashley's hand to leave, having suddenly remembered something she left in the car that required *immediate* attention, could see the collective shoulders of all the pharmacists, their backs to the counter, shaking with laughter. It took Leigh only about fifteen or twenty years to join in that laugh.

14

Find a Hole and Fill It

It has been my experience that small children have much stronger feelings about vacuums than does mere Nature—which purports to abhor them. One of the strongest human drives, more so than sex or the desire to edit another person's copy, is the need to put objects into holes. If a toddler finds a hole of any kind, the next thing he/she will do is find something to put in it. If another toddler finds a tiny object, he/she immediately *knows* with an inborn knowledge passed through centuries of DNA that *this* is Something Too Small for Me to Play With and as Soon as an Adult Realizes I've Got It, I'll Lose It So I Must Find a *Hole* to Put It In—*Now.*

It could be a tiny rock, and the first available hole might be a very small one that nobody has ever noticed before inside the dishwasher. They never noticed that little hole before because they are all giants and have to bend down to look inside the dishwasher and they are concerned only with whether or not the dishes inside are clean or dirty—and other related matters like who was supposed to fill it and who was supposed to run it and did they or not and who was supposed to empty it. They are not two feet tall and so they fail to appreciate the yawning cavern of the appliance and all the intricate features of its interior—like this little bitty hole that is just big enough to allow this little bitty rock to slip inside it.

They also don't know that if you put a little bitty rock inside that little bitty hole inside the dishwasher, you will get to see how many bubbles the dishwasher makes when the door is shut because they will all come out to play in the kitchen and some of them will even venture out into the family room and halfway down the hall. Dishwashers are probably *The* World's Champion Bubble Blowers, in case you're interested.

Yes, a real child did that with a real rock and a real dishwasher. The same child, when he was old enough to go out in the yard unsupervised for brief periods, managed, during one of those brief periods, to observe the two-inch elevation of the next-door neighbor's screenless window. Not only did he observe it, he hauled his own mama's garden hose over to it, fed the hose into the open window, and turned on the water—all before his mama called him to come inside for a sandwich, and I guess we all know how distracting a good sandwich can be. He clean forgot about his irrigation project. It was lucky that neighbor lady came home to cook supper and called to let his mama know how it all turned out. No, wait, maybe that wasn't so lucky after all. Man, those were some mad people.

Of course, many small items get put into the personal mouths of little kids. What parent has not had the thrilling experience of combing through a fully loaded diaper in search of a lost penny? Babies can and will swallow all manner of household items — but at least these attempts to eat the inedible make some sort of sense.

What *was* Queen Kim's three-year-old son thinking when he put that popcorn seed up his left nostril? Of course, "What were they thinking?" is the oldest and, to date, still unanswered question on the lips of every parent since Cain and Abel had that little dustup.

Many times, however, that question pops up (and remains unanswered) in the minds of Wives regarding their (Igmo) Husbands. Consider for a moment the husband of Kim — the father of little Johnny Popcornseed here. He is made aware of the fact that #1 Son has a kernel lodged in the port side of his proboscis. He observes that although #1 Son seems to be bearing up under this affliction quite well, #1 Wife, Kim, appears some the worse for the whole experience.

Family Problem Solver and Crisis Handler are two of the hats assigned to Husband — in his mind, at any rate. We would not expect that he would get Kim's vote in these areas, however — especially after the Orville Reden–Nostril Affair. Okay,

Igmo Dad somehow recalled that there was one of those snot syringe gizmos languishing in the medicine cabinet. Languishing would be all they're good for, but Igmo Dad believed he had hit upon a surefire, can't miss, *"really cool"* way to get the nugget out of #1's nose.

Does the name "Tim the Tool-Man" Taylor mean anything to ya? Oh, yeah. Igmo Dad watches too much TV. He, in all seriousness and with every intention of implementing it, took that baby snot syringe, hooked it up to his SHOP VAC, and came looking for Junior.

It would be a tough call to determine just who in this little family was more upset by the day's developments: Junior, the victim of a self-inflicted popcorn mishap, now forced to flee from his Shop-Vac-wielding dad; Kim, the mother of the victim of the self-inflicted popcorn mishap, now forced to aid and abet her son in his flight from his Shop-Vac-wielding dad—and also forced to realize that she gave birth to one-half of this duo and married the other half; or poor, dejected Dad, who went to all the trouble of thinking up and creating this fantastic Nasal Popcorn Retrieval Device and realizing that nobody in *this* house appreciates a *thing he does*.

It was a pretty rough-looking crew that pulled up to the emergency room that day. Junior still had a loaded Jiffy Pop up his snout that could blow at any moment; Kim was a wreck—just torn between two igmos (a condition common to all Married Mothers of Sons); and Dad was still convinced that his machine would have worked—"like a charm," I'm sure was the way he described it.

Two-thirds of the crew was visibly improved by exit time. Junior had two clear barrels; Kim was naturally relieved and cheered by this; Dad, on the other hand, was nearly suicidal when he realized that he just paid three hundred dollars to what looked like a ten-year-old doctor to fish out the popcorn kernel with a PAPER CLIP. Another miracle of modern medicine.

TammyLinda was driving along with her three-year-old son, Allen, in that blissfully ignorant state that mothers share— right before they notice in the rearview mirror that their son is shaking his head repeatedly from side to side and they ask him why is he doing that and he tells them it's because he has an *eye* in his *ear*—like, duhhh, how could she ask such a stupid question? And so she is then forced to ask yet another one along the lines of "What do you mean, you have an eye in your ear?" He patiently explains that he found one of those little googly doll eyes and he put it in his ear—again, like, duhhh—what else would one do? And she, just making conversation during the detour to the ER, asks ever Mom-like, "*Why* did you put it in your *ear?*" *Big duh . . . because he didn't have any pockets, Mom!*

I suppose moms would have an easier time understanding crap like this if they had started life as little boys—but then they'd be trying to hook the baby's nose up to the Shop-Vac, too. So, I guess it's worked out best in the long run with the current setup.

Loveys

Very often babies form überattachments to particular blankets, stuffed animals, pacifiers, and other regular baby-type merchandise. It is not unusual to see kindergarten-age children still wagging around a square of fabric that looks like it might have been on the losing side in the chariot races in *BEN-HUR*, and should the nasty thing go missing, the frenzy of the parents' search for it would be second only to what one would expect to see displayed if the actual CHILD were to disappear.

If your baby seems to be bonding with a particular object, it would behoove you to go out right that second and buy as many of whatever it is that you can find—and secretly wool them around to achieve and maintain an identical state of wear and general nastiness compared with the original—JUST IN CASE.

The Cutest Boy in the World and I were recently forced to

pass through LaGuardia Airport. I say "forced" because who can really stand to fly anywhere these days? If I could somehow transport myself to other locations by drinking modest amounts of drain cleaner or putting one or two fingertips in the garbage disposal, I'd take it over air travel any day. But anyway, we were endlessly waiting by the conveyor belt in baggage claim at LaGuardia and there was a darling young couple with their even darlinger little toddler girl-baby waiting even more endlessly—time does slow down when you're doing even regular stuff that annoys the crap out of everybody if you're having to do it with a baby added.

But this little baby girl seemed unperturbed by the lengthy wait and was happy to go from the tired arms of one parent to the other, over and over, as long as she had clutched in her tiny little hand this really awful-looking wad of . . . HAIR. Hmmmm. The darling young dad was holding the even darlinger little girl who was holding her icky hair wad as I caught his eye and said, "Mmmm, NICE HAIR!" The darling young mom came over and said, "Oh, mercy, it's her WIGLET and she will NOT let it go." I pointed out that, prolly in a few YEARS, they were really gonna regret that choice for a "lovey"—as it was already looking pret-ty awful. Darling Mom said, "Oh, believe me, WE did NOT choose it." Which, of course, I already knew—no parent would willingly set out to saddle themselves with a ratty hunk of travel hair as a love object for four or five years running.

As the bags came out and Darling Dad went to retrieve them, he set Darlinger Daughter down on the floor and she stood, only a tad wobbly, holding on to the upright handle of her very own little suitcase. She was only momentarily distracted by the task of remaining vertical and very soon noticed that her fuzzy lovey was not in her hand but rather sitting on top of Darling Mom's purse on the luggage cart.

The storm clouds began to form instantly but were just as quickly dispersed when the very alert Darling Mom reached over, snatched up the object of desire, and placed it in the outstretched hand of Darlinger Daughter. Baby girl was now COMPLETELY happy, all was absolutely right with her world, she was standing on her own two little feet, with a little help from her own little suitcase, and clutching her beloved hairball to her tiny bosom. It was easily the darlingest thing we'd seen all day—prolly all year.

I told the Darling couple that I was an author and that I had just that week finished my latest book—*The Sweet Potato Queens' Guide to Raising Children for Fun and Profit*—but that I was going back home to add in a chapter JUST FOR their very darling daughter, Ansley, and her precious wiglet—so here it is. Turned out they were from Hattiesburg, Mississippi, and had read my other books—proving what I always say, there are NO "degrees of separation" in the South!

Traveling with Kids

The number of people you are able to make miserable by traveling with your children is in direct correlation to your mode of travel. For example, if your company is made up of yourself and one child in an automobile, then the number of wretches is two—not counting, of course, the other people you'll encounter at gas stations and/or restaurants along the way. If you have yourself and your spouse and more than one child, the math works out the same way—just y'all and whatever random strangers you cross paths with en route.

It's when you jump over to public transportation that you can really produce some impressive numbers—a couple hundred at a whack on a big plane, plus everybody in the various airport terminals you move through. *Nobody* wants to see a bunch of strollers waiting at the gate check when they board the plane—because they know each of those little vehicles represents at least one baby-type person on that flight. And odds are good that at least one of those babies will be a nonstop screamer with inhuman volume and range.

I think the pharmaceutical companies could really win some loyal customers with a Free Drugs on Flights marketing campaign. Instead of sending their drug reps out with all those free samples to physicians' offices, how about sending a few boxcar-loads to the airlines? Hand out—in coach and first class alike—free Xanax, sleep masks, and earplugs to the adults and free Benadryl or Dramamine for everybody under eighteen. Just put the whole damn plane to sleep—I know the flight attendants would welcome it. If somebody tries to pass on the offer, the attendants should just smile big and put it in their beverage.

Queen Terri and her Spud Stud Bill were forced to make a cross-country flight with a three-year-old boy and a four-year-old girl, both of their own making. Bill did his part by making first-class reservations—God love him—and Terri brought the Dramamine—everybody on that plane was calling for God's Richest Most Abundant Blessings on Her.

The attendant came right out with some 7UP for the kids, and while Bill entertained them by pointing out all the various buttons there were that could be pushed and what would happen when you pushed 'em—like the flight attendant call button, always a crowd pleaser—Terri was surreptitiously mixing up the Mickeys to slip to the tots. Carefully stirring a dose of Dramamine into each 7UP, she signaled to Bill that the kids' drinks were ready, their own wine was waiting for them—let's all have a toast to a pleasant flight.

All would have been well had one of the children not caught the wink between Terri and Bill. The four-year-old immediately started yelling—as loud as she could, which, if you know any four-year-olds, you know is easily louder than any jet engine at full throttle—*"Oh, no! Please don't give us the sleeping medicine! Pleeeeease don't give us the sleeping medicine!"*

Terri froze—and that guilty expression on her face froze as well—very deer-in-the-headlights-ish—as literally every single head on every body in that plane turned in her direction and every eye looked until it settled on *her*—the drug-pusher mom.

Now, this is a conundrum of sorts we've got going here because all of these people are looking at her like she is Rasputin-Mom, poisoning her two children—and one of them is wise to it and begging for mercy as if it meant her very life. But those same people would be looking at her with equal loathing if, mid-taxi, her children began their cross-country screech-fest. Those people *want* her to drug those children—they want it *bad*—they want it like they want their next breath—but at the same time, they can't resist the chance to send withering glances her way for clumsily tipping off her victims to their fate.

Terri and Bill know all this wordlessly because, after all, they have had these kids for only four years—before that, *they*

145

were the ones passing out nasty looks to traveling families. Terri tries to look more reassuring than menacing and tries to convince her daughter that they aren't taking the "tummy medicine—because we're not riding in a car"—it's just 7UP. Sis can see that little brother has finished his and he's still vertical, ventilating, and verbalizing, so she finally gives in and chugs hers as well.

A peaceful flight was had by all and the well-rested children were a delight to all when the final destination was reached that night. Win/win. Terri said she was greatly reassured about her pharmaceutical intervention when she read in the very next month's issue of a major parenting magazine what we all know to be true: This is the only humane method for traveling with children—for them and for us. But how about you just try to work on that sleight of hand a little bit before you try to pull it off in public.

A Pulse Does Not a Babysitter Make

I do know full well just how important it is to spend time with our children—and I know even fuller and weller how absolutely *vital* it is to get *away* from them from time to time. The babysitting issue is just huge. I mean, you think twice before you let someone else drive your car—we're talking about your pearl beyond price here. Who're you gonna trust to hold it for a while?

Once Peep got to the stage of consuming foodstuffs that were not produced on the premises of my body, I hired a sitter to come to the house while I went to teach a class or two. This was working so well—I thought. Then one day, my down-the-street neighbor came by to tell me that he had driven by earlier and seen *my baby* in the park across the street—*by herself.* She walked quite well at nine months and he said that she appeared to be having herself a large time, toddling around the unoccu-pied swing set. He stopped the car—thank God—and re-trieved the little wanderer and walked over to my house, where the front door was standing wide open, giving him an easy view of the babysitter, flopped on the sofa, talking on the phone.

So that arrangement didn't last too long. Didn't last much past my conversation with the neighbor, actually.

Granted, the more time wears on and the more worn out we become, the better just about *any* babysitter will look to us. *Good Dog, Carl* is our favorite fantasy. (If you're unfamiliar with that book, go get it—you'll see what I mean. Rottweiler as care-giver.)

Queen Pam had a built-in bevy of babysitters right across the hall—beer-drinking, sports-on-TV-loving lawyers. All she had to do was chill a case of brews, show 'em where Baby Gen's bottles were and remind them how to warm 'em up for her, turn on the game, and she and her hubby had instant date night. (I'm assuming these were brand-new lawyers, still paying off student loans, who couldn't afford beer, let alone a television.) The lawyers were an efficient bunch of sots. They figured out that the baby's Portacrib would fit perfectly under the glass-top coffee table, so that's where they would park little Gen during the games. Every time they reached for their beers, there would be the smiling/sleeping/crying baby, in plain sight—and only one of those scenarios required any action from them. I wonder if Gen will go to law school one day.

That lawyerly bunch apparently had some kind of coffee-table theme going. They were at somebody else's house drinking one night, and when an exceptionally short member of the crew passed out on the floor in the middle of the room, the others simply rolled him under the wooden coffee table in order to keep the pathway to the beer cooler navigable. They went home and forgot him—or perhaps they forgot him and then went home—in any case, he was left under the low, heavy wooden table. When he opened his eyes the next morning, he nearly had a heart attack—and his bellowing nearly gave everybody else in the house one as well. It wasn't until he swung his arms out to the side that he realized that he was *not* buried alive. Of course, he's a judge today.

My precious darlin' George was left in the care of his very own daddy—and can we all agree that it is *not* "babysitting" if the person doing the sitting is also the one who did the "fathering"? He is the baby-daddy, and as such he has parenting responsibilities—much like those of the baby-mama—and those responsibilities frequently call for the parent in question to be left in full charge of the baby—with no assistance from other persons. A "babysitter" is a person who is temporarily taking care of a child not of that person's own creation. A babysitter can be a friend, grandmother, grandfather, aunt, uncle, cousin, neighbor—any*body* but the child's father. If the male parent of a child is the sole parent in charge for any period of time, he is on *Dad Duty*—he is *not* babysitting. Can you imagine a *mother* ever saying to her girlfriend, "No, I can't go out, I'm babysitting the kids tonight"? No, of course not, *they're her kids.*

Okay, so—we've got Little George—left in the care of Big George. So what does Big George do but take Little George *duck hunting.* I'm not sure how old Little George was at this time, but you should understand that in the South, children often have their own firearms before they have any permanent teeth. From the sound of this story, I'd say Little George was young enough that he knew he had no choice but to go—but old enough to know he'd rather be set on fire. In the telling of it, he makes it sound like *so* much fun—"Get there while it's still dark, hide, be still, wait, freeze, and shoot ducks." (Sure makes me wanna go.)

Somehow, four ducks were killed—one of which nearly killed them in return by falling on them. The other three landed off in the icy-cold, flooded backwaters of Steele Bayou, and Big George, according to Little George, "being too cheap for either boat or dog, elects *me* to strip down to my scanties and play retriever." Little George will not eat duck to this day.

Parents who leave their younger children under the supervision of their older children must be prepared to field constant two-way tattling phone calls. Of all the pitiful child-care options available to us, this one seems the least desirable to me on account of there's no relief. Even though we probably really do *need* to know what is going on in our absence, we really don't *want* to know. If we don't know, we can at least enjoy the peace and quiet and *pretend* to ourselves for just a little while that all is well at home.

When you've got big siblings bossing little siblings, not only do you not have any peace and quiet but you are kept *up to the minute* on every single transgression of everybody in the house all day long. You might as well be there refereeing the melee yourownself.

Big Sis Jennifer (thirteen) was home alone with nine-year-old Melissa. It was not going particularly well, but neither was there any bloodshed, which could be called a total victory in some families. Presently, however, Jennifer discovered that Melissa had betaken herself out onto the roof of the house, and when asked, then told, then yelled at, to come down from there this very instant, Melissa, of course, flatly refused, buried her nose in a book, and pretended she could no longer hear the shouts of her sister.

Jennifer finally felt she had no choice and she informed Melissa of this — she was going inside To Call Mother at Work. The call did not come at a particularly good time for Mom. She was, after all, at *work* and therefore *doing things* that required her full attention, which was captured at once by her older daughter when she heard the lead-in, the requisite "MO-O-O-OM" in the unmistakable and universal tone of the tattler, followed by "Melissa's on the ro-of and she won't come do-own."

After the briefest hesitation where we imagine she was tempted to slam the phone down and race home to beat the crap out of both of them, she asked the very pertinent question, "Well, what is she *doing* on the roof?" Jennifer replied, "She *says* she's doing her math homework."

Mom, who was just teetering on the brink, said, "Well, if she's doing homework, leave her ass up there." You really do have to learn to be very selective about your battles.

Kids' Parties

If you're like me—and I strongly suspect that you are—then you would rather stab yourself in the eye with a green pinecone than be forced to throw a birthday party for a bunch of kids. However, in an informal poll of a random sampling of children of varying ages, temperaments, economic backgrounds, and ethnicities—oh, who'm I kidding—I didn't ask a single kid, didn't have to—I already *know* without asking that, given the choice between watching us stab ourselves in the eyeball with the unripe fruit of a conifer and having themselves a birthday party, the little shits are gonna pick the party *every damn time.* I think it's possible that they might consider the swap if they were allowed to do the eye-jabbing themselves, but it doesn't seem like a really viable alternative. After all, we have only the two eyeballs to sacrifice—four, if we have a participatory spouse—and the birthdays roll around every single year. Clearly, after just a few short years, it would be necessary to sacrifice some other equally important personal body part, and by the time you got the kid through adolescence, you would be, at best, half the person you were when you started, which may not serve you well over the rest of your life.

I read with interest and something very like awe a book called *The Children's Party Book,* put out by the Junior League of Hampton Roads, Inc. If I didn't think the Leaguers were the hardest-working women on the planet *before,* this little book cemented my belief. That any of them had time to even think this stuff up—what with all the regular 24/7/365 League work they're already doing—and then go to all the trouble of putting it into a book—well, no wonder the rest of us are such slackasses—these women have sucked all the energy out of the universe for themselves. Each community should harness up a few Leaguers to some kind of treadmill to generate electricity—we could be oil-free in no time.

There are no Beta Moms in any Junior League, anywhere— it was started by Alpha Moms—even though those terms were invented only last week, the two types have existed since moms were invented—and only *Alphas* are even *considered* for membership. Which is fine by us Betas, we're not the least bit miffed by the exclusion. I shudder to think of the carnage should a hapless *Beta* somehow find herself in the ranks of the League—

being fined into bankruptcy would be the most pleasant aspect of her fate.

Alpha Moms will love *The Children's Party Book*—and will no doubt think of many additional "fun" and labor-intensive things to do for each party. *Beta* Moms will think it's a joke book. There are in this book no fewer than twenty-five different party themes for birthday and holiday celebrations—all of which are apparently intended to occur in one's own home, and that right there is the absolute death kiss on the deal for me.

Never allow into your home—for any reason short of some sort of mass emergency-evacuation situation that would necessitate the humanitarian harboring of large numbers of children in one's personal space—more than one additional child over and above the number that normally lives there every day. If you happen to have more than one child under your personal care and roof, you should discourage them from having friends at all—sooner or later, it will only lead to in-home visitation. Bound to happen.

Should you just have the one little chicken in your nest, it is okay to allow him/her to have multiple friends so long as they only congregate at your house one at a time. This is especially true if you happen to have a girl-type child. Boys apparently can play together just fine in groups of just about any number—they are guaranteed to do stupid things but at least all are allowed equal opportunity for participating in the stupidity. But it is an immutable law of the universe—it's prolly in the

Bible somewhere even—that while two little girls may play happily together for indefinite periods of time, the simple addition of one more little girl completes the disaster recipe.

It's like the way fires start—as long as there's an element missing, nothing burns, but once you stick that missing piece in there, it's Smokey Bear time. You put three little girls in a room together and you *will* have a roaring two-against-one conflagration about *something* in short order.

Another reason to *not* have a child's party on your own premises is that by doing so, you are putting yourself 100 percent at the nonexistent mercy of Other Parents. At least a few of these fiends will read your invitation with a wicked cackle, RSVP their acceptance within nanoseconds, and begin planning how they are going to while away the hours of their beester-free afternoon/evening, courtesy of *you*. Oh, it doesn't matter if you plainly state on the invite that the party is from two to four p.m.—they won't come back until they are good and ready. And face it, you've met their kid—how good and ready would *you* be to reclaim that beester?

They know that you will be doing the headless-chicken-run with a houseful of hellions, no way you can answer your telephone, and so they'll call and leave you a breathless voice mail to let you know how *terribly* sorry they are for what they know is just going to be the worst possible imposition, but they have been somehow unavoidably detained and they're afraid their cell phone is about to die, so they'll have to call you back just as soon as they . . . Silence. And you'll know you have Been Had.

There are some unscrupulous parents who will pull the ole drop-and-run maneuver on you no matter where you have the gathering—they don't object at all to their little beester going home with you for a few hours after Chuck E. Cheese closes. Once painful experience has identified them, you can attempt to thwart them the next time by asking them to help chaperone the event, but you shouldn't pat yourself on the back too hard just because they've agreed to do it. Doesn't mean they *will*. Doesn't mean they won't get an "urgent" call right in the middle of the deal that "forces" them to have to leave early—and then provides them with the perfect excuse to also be late for the postparty beester retrieval. These people are incorrigible.

The only thing you can do about them really is to make absolutely *certain* that you are at least three hours late picking your child up from *their* party—oh, and the perfect birthday gift for their little beester? A drum set and a live monkey—a tad expensive, possibly, but totally worth it, don't you think?

The Tooth Fairy
and Other Skulduggery

The Tooth Fairy was very much persona non grata at my house when BoPeep began parting with that first set of pearly whites. Easily an entire month's worth of drama was devoted to that very first loose tooth. Much of that month Peep spent in front of a mirror, wiggling the little fanglet and grimacing to see the effects of the wiggling. When *would* that tooth *ever* come out? That was the hourly question.

Peep's best friend, Kate, lived three doors down, and since they were the only two kids on the whole entire street, they were pretty much inseparable. I'll never forget the anticipation that the prospect of our moving in held for the four-year-old Kate, who had lived as the only person under forty on the whole street her whole life until then. She was absolutely *wild* with excitement, and whenever she would see me or MoonPie down at the house, she would race over to ask if we were "moving in *today*??" When at *last* that long-awaited move-in day did arrive, Kate saw the trucks, followed by our car, shouted to her mom, Rita, *"My little girl is here! My little girl is here!"* and out the door she flew, wingless—carried aloft by sheer delight—to our front door.

From then on they were, as I said, pretty much inseparable and, it should also be noted, not a little competitive. As it happened, Kate did *not have* a loose tooth at that particular time, but she did have some very fine and quite expensive crowns on some baby teeth, so, with a great deal of grit and determination, she managed to loosen one of those, much to the chagrin of her hardworking, dental-bill-paying parents.

Then, the fateful moment finally arrived. It became perfectly clear that our tooth was going to make its exit any second now. Peep freaked. After four weeks of endless tooth-wiggling and nagging me about when it would come out—now that it was actually happening, she simply could not deal. *"I'm not ready! I'm not ready!"* she wailed.

I suggested she just go sit quietly on the big white sofa in the den—right by the mirror—wait for the Moment and all would be well. Miraculously, she did as I prompted, and, even more miraculously, it happened just as I predicted. With no strings tied to doorknobs, no pulling, no prodding, it fell out of its own accord—a perfectly pain-free, bloodless coup. We were pret-ty proud of ourselves, too. On the phone in a flash, she was, calling Kate to boast.

A very drained Rita, mother to Kate, phoned me later in the day to report the grisly scene that unfolded at her house when the news of Peep's tooth reached there. It seemed that Kate had no more than hung up the phone when she seized that cap on her front tooth and commenced to twisting and yanking on it with an adult-sized vengeance, yowling all the while. She was bound and determined to have that tooth extracted before Peep could walk down the street to display her new gap.

When she was unsuccessful, there was hell to pay and only Rita to foot the bill, bless her heart. It took no small amount of cajoling and probably some fairly expensive bribery to soothe the still fully-toothed Kate.

Rita then demanded to know what damage that bitch Tooth Fairy was going to be inflicting on us all—knowing all too well that, as the loser of the first tooth in the neighborhood, we would be setting the unshakable precedent. "Well," I told her, "somehow Peep has become fixated on the idea of 'hundred-dollar bills.'" *"OHGODNO!"* was the explosion on the other end of the line.

I allowed as how, first of all, I had no earthly idea where Peep even *heard* of the mythic "hundred-dollar bill," since there had never been one at *our* house that I knew about, and furthermore, since they had not sprouted on any of the trees in my yard, I didn't see how it was possible that the Tooth Fairy was gonna produce one, even for this very fine tooth.

Rita heaved what can only be described as an *extra large*

sigh of relief. But that did plant the seed of an *extra large* diabolical thought in my own brain. I could rig a deal with Rita— price-fixing the Tooth Fairy—with a kickback. She could pay *me* twenty dollars for every tooth Kate lost, and for that consideration, I would agree to set the Tooth Fairy premium at five dollars per tooth—and friend Rita would be *saving* seventy-five dollars per! Surely, she would see the enormous value in this?

I decided that the friendship, goodwill, and babysitting I shared with Rita were far more valuable to me than this measly profit, however, so I shelved the scheme. But I was still in a quandary about the Tooth Fairy Toll. What to do? What to do?

Here is my child, my heart, my only one—yearning and hoping and somehow almost believing that she *is* going to get a "hundred-dollar bill" for her little tooth. And over here is the purse of the Tooth Fairy, with nary a "hundred-dollar bill" inside. I am torn between that precious, earnest little face—and very harsh Reality.

I mean, I'm calculating that she's got around twenty teeth that are gonna come out in the coming months and I don't exactly have an extra couple of grand to blow on teeth that are not even usable anymore. So I compromised.

The Tooth Fairy came up with twenty bucks—with an accompanying note explaining that even *this* amount, while admittedly not a "hundred-dollar bill," was still an *exorbitant* sum for a tooth. (Even at that tender age, Peep knew words like "exorbitant," thanks mostly to my seester, Judy, who taught her to say "ratatouille" and "bouillabaisse" before she was two. It was always pretty entertaining for Judy when Peep would say them around people who were thrilled their kid had finally mastered "da-da.")

The note went on to remind Peep that the Tooth Fairy does service the *en*-tire planet and kids are losing teeth at a pretty fair clip. This ridiculously high amount was awarded as a meritorious tribute to Peep's bravery and to commemorate the loss of this, the very first little tooth. (All this in hopes of being able to trade down for subsequent teeth.)

A few weeks passed and eventually Kate was finally able to pry that crown out of her mouth, and the Tooth Fairy visited their house as well—to the tune of, you guessed it, twenty bucks, and Rita was just dog-cussing me the whole time.

A few more weeks passed and Peep had a second tooth loosening. We followed the same drill—wiggling, grimacing, nagging about the time line, until fall-out was imminent—and then it was a repeat performance of the whole *"I'm not ready! I'm not ready! NOT READY!"* deal. She once again goes and sits on the sofa by the mirror, and once again it plops out on its own.

And again with the haggling over money—all day long she is tormenting me, "I just *know* she's gonna bring me a hundred-dollar bill *this* time." If I heard it once, I heard it fifteen hundred times that day, and each time I would say, "Now, darlin', I just don't want you to be disappointed—she is *not* going to bring you a hundred dollars—she just isn't. The Tooth Fairy is just a very small fairy and she is very low in the hierarchy of the whole realm of fairy-dom—no way she's got that kind of budget—Santa Claus would not hear of it."

But all day long it continued—Peep voicing her heartfelt little hopes and me dashing them in as consoling a way as I could find and getting nowhere. As dark approached, I was fairly panic-stricken, since all my talking had not slowed her down one whit in her relentless pursuit of the elusive "hundred-dollar bill." Once more at bedtime, she said to me, "Oh, I hope, I hope, I *hope* she brings me a hundred-dollar bill!" and one more time I tried gently but firmly to throw the cold water of reality on that hope.

Finally, clearly exasperated, she growled, *"Mom!"* and she pulled me down close so she could utter this piercing whisper in my ear: *"I'm just trying to get another twenty-dollar bill here—will you please be quiet?"*

I just lost it—we are trying to *trick* the Tooth Fairy? She knew perfectly well that twenty dollars a tooth was a ridiculous amount of money. She *knew* it *all along* and she worked it like the pro she already was. And I am here to tell you, she *absolutely* got that twenty-dollar bill—a scam that perfectly crafted and conducted *deserved* to succeed.

Kids' Cussing

Now, y'all know, if you have read any of my other books (and I certainly hope that you have or soon will), that my language would practically qualify me to be the Admiral of all the Navies. I cuss. A lot. I admit that I began the practice as an early adolescent as a surefire means of irritating the shit (see, there I go) out of my own personal mother, and I can tell you that I was 100 percent successful 100 percent of the time.

I was so successful and enjoyed it so very much that it became what is apparently an unshakable habit to this very day. And I assure you, it *still* irritates the shit outta MawMaw.

My daddy's theory—to which I ascribe—was that there is No Such Thing as a Bad Word. Humans made up every single word there is, and likewise, we assigned each one a meaning, and they are all *just words*. Daddy had assorted parables to illustrate his various policies regarding language.

For instance, name-calling—that cherished playground tradition. Whenever we would run, bawling, to him with the report that "Brindy called me a butthead," he would look at us calmly and question the veracity of the statement. "*Are* you a butthead?" And we would sob loudly in the negative, to which he would then raise the question, "Well, what if she called you a chair. You're not a chair either, are you?" This would usually cause us to stop mid-wail and look confused. He would go on to explain that both are just words—and as long as we could be certain that we were not, in fact, doing anything either buttheaded or chairlike, it didn't much matter what Brindy called us in a fit of temper.

Little seven-year-old Zoe rushed in from the neighborhood kickball game to report to her mama that one of the boys had been calling her nasty names. Mama Rosie asked just what particular nasty names had been flung at her baby girl. "*White Girl,*" Zoe sobbed. Rosie had to catch the laugh that sprang to her lips as she pointed out the obvious to her daughter—that being that Zoe *was*, in fact, a girl and was also clearly white—so wherein exactly did the insult lie?

Zoe reported that the epithet had been delivered in a mean tone of voice, accompanied by some other words, leaving her doubtless as to the underlying intent. What other words, her mama asked. "Well, "bitch," for one," but no tears accompanied this revelation. Rosie pondered on the fact that her daughter was devastated at being called a white girl in a derogatory tone but was completely unfazed at the bitch label.

Zoe explained that it hurt her feelings for her friend to slam her for being two things she had no choice about—white and female—that was just plain mean, but since she had strong opinions about stuff and wasn't afraid to stand up for what she believed, she figgered she was gonna get called "bitch" a whole lot in her life.

God love her, I hope little Zoe—yes, and all of us and all our girls, too—get called "bitch" till the end of time.

Daddy's parable relating to "words being just words" was the one about the Slob Housewife, the Neat Freak Husband, and the Very Dusty Coffee Table. OOOOOH, Mr. Neat Freak Man, he couldn't *stand* that dusty table, nosiree, it just about drove him crazy. (Now, I always wanted to know, if it bothered him so dang much, how come he didn't just *dust* the sumbitch? But this is not really a story about dust after all.)

In his anguish over the dusty table, he decides that the Thing to Do is to just write "I love you" in the dust—thinking in his furtive little passive-aggressive brain that she will first read the "love" note, but then realize just how very dusty the table is and be moved to deal with it and all will be well.

Now, if I came home and found such a note, I'd be sizing up his ass to determine just how far up it I could shove that dusty table—but that's just me. And, it must be said, our Slob Housewife wasn't exactly feeelin' the luuuuv either. I imagine that she wrestled inwardly for a good moment or two before taking what I believe to be the very highest road available to her—a totally weapon-free response—she simply wrote her own message next to his, in the very deep dust on the table, "I love you, too!"

Daddy's point was that although there was no such thing as a "bad" word, there was such a thing as "bad" *intent* and there was plenty of it around, too. This couple, he said, had chosen their *words* very carefully—attempting to put an innocent face on the malevolent message each wished to impart. Did either one of them *mean* that they were loving the other one at that moment? No, they did not. Did either one of them believe for an instant that they were receiving a loving message from their spouse? No, they most assuredly did not.

Daddy always thought that if God was judging anything, He was prolly smart enough to tell the difference between what came out of our mouths and what was truly in our hearts. I thought that made a lot of sense and still do. My mama has never shared this view, however, and I can assure you, she is Properly Horrified at my language, and if you were to meet her, within five minutes of the introduction she would somehow work it into the conversation that I "didn't learn all that at home." And she's right about that.

But I know of at least a few kids who *did* learn a whole bunch of really good "bad" words at home or real close by, and it was pretty entertaining to watch as they tried them out for the first time.

Little Bryanna had been spending some summer-vacation time on her uncle Stan's farm and she felt very grown up about "helping work the cattle," giving her mama detailed descriptions of dehorning and all manner of other farmy stuff, and her mama was tickled that she was learning so many new things. When Mama came to fetch little Bryanna, there was still much activity going on in the cow area and no one saw her arrive. Mama walked down to the pens just in time for some minor drama as a cow got out of the chute and made a break for it. Imagine Mama's less-than-delighted surprise when she saw dainty little Bryanna take out after the bovine, bellowing, *"You Goddamn sonofabitch, I'll kill you!"* No doubt Mama was thinking something along those lines as she approached the very sheepish Uncle Stan.

Sometimes they mean well. Tammy had herself a spa day while her three kids were playing at a friend's house—I'd call that a *very good* friend, myself. Anyway, the friend had a whole bunch of cats, and so, of course, at least one of the kids stepped in some poop on the way to the car when Tammy came to retrieve them. Such a rude ending to her very pleasant day. The car was immediately suffused in unbearable stink. Jacob, then four, soberly asked his mama if *crap* was a "bad" word. Tammy replied that, well, it wasn't a *nice* word. Jacob thought briefly and said, "Well, okay, then—your car smells like cat shit."

One really good friend of mine—we'll just call her "Ra-mona"—had her a pretty good potty mouth—not as pro-nounced as my own, of course, but, then, you hardly ever find that outside the confines of a boys' locker room or a deer camp. Amazingly enough, I've never been in either of those even though it prolly does sound like I was raised in one or the other.

Anyway, Ramona was known to let fly with regularity, and her husband and baby-daddy, Chip, was concerned that their toddler daughter, "O," was going to pick it up and parrot it back at some inopportune moment. Ramona's usual response was to meekly agree to Chip's face and vow to clean it up a bit. Although now and then, he would deliver his mini-lecture at a particularly irritating moment at the end of a particularly long and crabby day, and she would laugh to herself and flip him off behind his back. Nonetheless, he'd messed it up for her—whenever she had a satisfying stream of invective flowing, she'd remember his cau-tionary words—and it wouldn't slow her down much but it did throw off her rhythm. This was vexing to her.

One really hot, errand-filled day, she and Baby O had had just about enough of the heat and each other, but Ramona had completed all her tasks, gotten O buckled into her car seat for the umpteenth time that day, and settled into her own seat and cranked up the AC for the ride home. Before the inside temp had fallen much below the boiling point, O put up a holler that her baby doll, Hannah, had fallen to the floorboard and *Hannah couldn't ride on the floor—Hannah liked to look out the window!*

Ramona nearly wrenched her back trying to stretch far enough over the seat to retrieve the errant doll—and avoid having to open the car door to the blast furnace outside one more time. She could touch the hem of the doll's dress but she couldn't quiiiiite get a grip on it, so, seething with irritation and sweating like the pig she was sure was her scent-double, she flung open her door, lurched out into the parking lot, yanked open the rear door, snatched Hannah up, and thrust her into the outstretched hands of Baby O, who seized the doll by both arms, squeezing tightly and hissing at her through clenched teeth, "*Hannah!* You are just worryin' the fuckin' shit outta me!" in an absolutely FLAWLESS—albeit unintentional—impersonation of . . . someone.

Clearly, CLEARLY, Baby O had heard those words *somewhere* before—she even got the inflection right and everything. Ramona drove home through alternating waves of convulsive laughter and dread. I imagine she spent the next few hours plotting various ways to annoy Chip enough to force those same words from his lips before he heard little O say them—so he could then be blamed for the child's fulmination—and my money's on Ramona, for sure. Poor Chip—but he shoulda known the job was dangerous when he took it.

Erring on the side of caution, Queen Robbi's three-year-old daughter sought a parental ruling prior to letting fly one Sunday morning while standing in line with her mama waiting to shake the preacher's hand after the service. "Mommy, are we allowed to say 'goddamn it' in church?" The mortified Robbi responded, "No, baby, we don't say 'daddy words' in church." (If he'd wanted to defend himself against the charge, he shoulda been there—everybody knows, the absent parent gets blamed for any and all questionable behavior.)

"Daddy words" were a source of entertainment and not a little confusion in my childhood home. Daddy was always making up words for things and using them in normal conversation so that they sounded to us like real words. For example: A man up the street from us, Floyd, was a major ham radio aficionado with a garage crammed to the rafters with all manner of equipment. If there were people on Mars, Floyd was talking to 'em— there was no country on Earth he couldn't reach.

This was in the early fifties, when TV was in its infancy and absolutely anything could disrupt the reception. Everybody's sets had rabbit-ear antennae, usually with aluminum foil wrapped around the tips for some reason that is lost to me now, but it had something to do with improving reception by blocking out evil alien rays. However, even heavy-duty Reynolds Wrap could not defeat a massive ham radio two doors up the street.

The whole family watched TV together every night after supper. *I've Got a Secret* and *To Tell the Truth* were two favorites. Invariably, right at the moment of some Big Reveal Moment in our evening's entertainment, the television would start buzzing and the whole screen would be covered in black fuzzy lines.

Loud wails and groans would spout from every mouth and Daddy would calmly say, "Well, I guess ole Floyd's playing with his hoo-dad-lum again." I was probably fifteen before I realized that "hoodadlum" did NOT mean "ham radio."

One afternoon, my friend Janie's husband, Tom, came home from work, and their next-door neighbor accosted him and demanded that Tom pay for the wanton destruction of his car. This was a helluva homecoming for Tom, who had no earthly idea what the guy was talking about nor why he, Tom, should be expected to be financially responsible for whatever it was, and he said as much to his neighbor. Neighbor then suggested that Tom accompany him to view the wreck that had formerly been his car, and so Tom went with him and he readily admitted that the car was, in fact, a complete mess—dented and scratched all over, broken windows and mirrors—but he wondered aloud why it might be that the neighbor felt that this had anything to do with him, Tom, since he, Tom, had just that second driven home from work, where he had been all day long. Rock-solid alibi for ole Tom regarding the damaged vehicle.

Neighbor informed Tom that his, Tom's, children were responsible, and Tom said that somehow he doubted that, since his, Tom's, children were only three and five, respectively. Nonetheless, neighbor insisted that those very same kids were the culprits. Tom said he would certainly explore the matter further, and he betook his work-weary self into the house where, in one instant, two things registered in his brain. His eyes told him, first, that the aforementioned two little children who had been watching out the window were now scampering down the hall at warp speed, and next—that at least some of the contents of the large container of screw-top Gallo on the kitchen table were most likely inside his wife, Janie, and her best buddy, Pat.

Pouring himself a glass, he casually mentioned that the next-door neighbor was claiming that the children had torn up his car and he wanted to be paid for the damage. Janie and Pat declared, no way—the children had been perfect angels all afternoon long and had been playing together happily outside, without even a single quarrel requiring motherly intervention for several hours. Hmmmmm, Tom thought to himself, while a sense of foreboding and portents of body-shop bills settled around him like a cloak.

Pat decided her own hungry husband was probably about to arrive home, so she went on off to attend to that as Tom was summoning the young scallywags from their hiding places. "Oh, shit," was heard from down the hall, and that set Tom to thundering for them to present themselves and be quick about it. The car question was momentarily forgotten. Such language from his children! As they stood before him, clearly guilty of all manner of crimes and misdemeanors, he told them he was shocked, appalled, and dismayed at hearing such a word from one of them. After all, he said, they didn't hear *him* using such language, did they? No, sir, they replied. And they didn't hear *their mother* using such language, did they? (Sensing the direction this was taking, Janie had circled behind him and was making cut-throat gestures at them, broadly hinting at the destruction that might possibly befall them if they ratted her out.) We-e-e-e-lll—was all they could answer—not sure which to dread more, telling a fib to their father or finking on their mom—your basic rock and reeeally hard place.

Quick-thinking Janie—screw-top Gallo notwithstanding—recalled for Tom and the little rat finks the initial reason for this inquisition: the mysterious driveway demolition derby that had apparently been going on next door, and *who* had any information they wanted to share with the group about *that*?

Oh, yeah. That. What about that? Tom recounted for the group the tale of woe their neighbor had vented on him earlier and voiced his disbelief that his own two very young children could have been in any way responsible for such destruction of another's property, and Janie chimed in that she, too, was convinced of their innocence and further voiced her pride in them for having played together so well all afternoon while she and her friend Pat had such a lovely visit.

But, the two trusting parents asked, did either of the two little angels have any idea what *could* have happened to Mr. Neighbor Man's car—did they see anything, hear anything, that might be helpful in the solution of this mystery? The shifty little baby eyes and shuffling of the tiny feet did little to enhance their attempts at appearing innocent and unaware, and they were most reluctant to accompany their parents outside to survey the scene of the crime, and they reeeeally didn't want to see Mr. Neighbor Man—like, ever again in this life, even. Indeed, it seemed they weren't even the slightest bit *curious* about what might have transpired—they were quite ready and willing, desperate, if you will, to change the subject—even the prior conversation about bad language held a more promising outcome for them than this one.

That's when Tom knew he'd just bought himself a tore-up car.

While Janie, Pat, and Mr. Gallo had been enjoying one another's pleasant company, in the quiet afternoon absence of the normal din of children's quarreling, the two erstwhile angels had somehow run afoul of Mr. Neighbor Man. Who knows what happened? He probably told them to quit trampling his flower beds or something else that would sound quite reasonable to an adult but was enough to transform him forever in their young minds into a full-fledged, card-carrying, fire-breathing, puppy-kicking ogre—who needed to be Taught a Lesson.

Their "reasoning" was that he would never know it was the two of *them* who taught him this lesson—he would never know *what* happened or *how*—but he *would be sorry.* Typical Kid Logic. And how handy that there was a goodly-sized pile of broken bricks just sitting right there in the side yard, waiting to be hauled off—or, even better, flung at Mr. Ogre Man's car. I bet ole Tom did say "Shit" that night when the truth finally came out—even if the young'uns didn't hear it.

Never Underestimate How Hard a Little Kid Can Throw a Brick. Or several dozen.

Thou Wart-Necked Fat-Kidneyed Pignut

If you make a big-ass deal over your kid's cussing, I can pretty much guarantee you will get a whole lot more of it. I am living proof of this. No amount of soap and/or red pepper could curb my tongue. Rather than just resigning yourself to a four-letter future with your fourteen-year-old, I do have what I think is a most excellent solution. *Encourage* cursing. Absolutely *insist* that your little cussbox learn to do it with great flair and proficiency—by studying Shakespearean curses—like the one leading this section.

I think you'll find that most youngsters have about as much comprehension of the meaning of the currently popular four-letter words as they do of the fancy multisyllablic selections of the Bard—that is, zero. Four-year-old Bryan could not wait to tattle on his six-year-old sister, Michelle, for saying "the *B* word." He delivered the news in hushed tones but with that decidedly smug look behind the eyes that indicates extreme pleasure at the possibility of bringing down parental wrath upon the head of a sibling.

Michelle entered the room just in time to overhear—what a coincidence. She vehemently denied having said "the *B* word," and Bryan, of course, insisted just as staunchly that she *had*, in fact, *said it*. And so they went back and forth, to and fro, and Mom could take it no more and told them *both* to hush. The silence lasted for a small portion of a split second before Bryan muttered under his breath, "She did too say the *B* word," and, of course, this required a responsive mutter from Michelle, "Did not." This ushered in a chorus of "did/did not/did too/nuh-uh/uh-huh" and could have quickly deteriorated into severe name-calling, Ten Commandment–invoking, pinching, slapping, and hair-pulling had not Mom thrown in the towel and said, "*Fine*, just what '*B* word' is it that Michelle supposedly said, Bryan?" With a triumphant glaze over his face, he looked Michelle square in the eye as he ratted her out to Mama. "Michelle said '*Bagina*' and I heard her!"

Renee owns a day-care center, and she and another teacher were monitoring the four-year-olds out on the playground one afternoon when a little girl came running up to report the earth-shattering news that "Jack had said a *very bad* word." Is that so, Renee asked, which word is that? It was revealed that Jack had uttered "the *E* word," and this was most perplexing to Renee and her coworker—both full-grown, well-educated women—who, in all their travels, life experiences, and studies, had never, in their collective recollections, come across *any* so-called "bad" word beginning with the letter *e*. They scrolled mentally through the whole alphabet, reciting to each other in giggly whispers every cuss word they could think up, and neither of them could produce a single questionable word for the *e* category.

They were finally reduced to asking the child what the word was, and it took a good bit of coaxing and finally a gentle demand that she tell them exactly what the offensive *e* word was (if for no other reason than for their own edification and possible future use), and the child, with a very sober expression, looked both ways before she leaned in and whispered to them, "Jack said E-diot." "Idiot"—which, when you think about it, can be a very bad and most hurtful word, but it's not likely to get your mouth swabbed with soap in even the most conservative homes, and isn't *that* interesting?

Full-grown people can be such E-diots when it comes to "bad words," I swear. When my nephew Trevor was a tyke, he took piano lessons from a very prim middle-aged woman in the Garden District in New Orleans. One day, my seester, Judy, got a phone call from the teacher informing her that Trevor had been sent home—and would not be welcomed back—due to "bad language." What in the world could an eight-year-old boy have uttered that was so shocking and offensive to an adult as to result in expulsion? After much verbal wrangling with the woman, Judy finally wrung it out of her. "Your son," the woman reported, tight-lipped, "said a four-letter word That Starts with *F* and Ends in *T* and means *poot*!" Judy dropped the phone laughing and greeted Trevor at the door with the happy news that he would never have to return to the igmo piano teacher's house again in this life. What person over the age of five could really say with a straight face that they believe the word "poot" to be somehow more socially acceptable than "fart"?

There are numerous Web sites devoted to the subject—plop the little trash talker down in front of the computer and require him to write and learn what it means to call someone a "mewling sheep-bited maggot-pie" and/or a "gleeking hasty-witted hedge-pig." Actually, as I write, this is starting to appeal to me for my own personal use. I'm thinking the next time I encounter an individual who is, by their every word and deed, demanding to be addressed most sharply, I will cast a fiery glare in their direction and inform them that I believe that they—and all their ancestors—are nothing more than fishified toad-spotted clotpoles, and I expect it will feel rather satisfying.

Hey, this could be an answer to all those vile rap lyrics, yes? Seems to me that "Yo, yo—pukin' beef-witted wagtail" couldn't be any harder to rhyme than "gittin' out my bitch stick."

Fulminating for Fun and Fostering Fine Feelings

When my dear friend Paul was but a wee lad and his brother Joe was even wee-er, they found themselves sitting, bored, on the curb in front of their home. As often happens when small boys are left to their own devices, one of them had an Idea. Naturally, it was the big brother, Paul, who had the idea for what the little brother, Joe, should do. Paul thought it would be highly entertaining to everyone for miles around if Joe was to see just *how loud* he could yell the word "butthole."

Joe, of course, thought that any idea emanating from his older, wiser, infinitely cooler big brother was unadulterated genius, and he agreed excitedly to give it his very best try—which he did and which, of course, Paul found woefully inadequate. Over and over, the little brother would yell *"Butthole!"* as loud as he thought he could, and each time, Paul would cock his head, dutifully listen, and, after a few moments of thoughtful consideration, pronounce that it was *some* better, but still not qui-i-i-ite the volume that he, Paul, found desirable and truly believed that Joe was capable of producing if he gave it the ole 110 percent try.

So finally, for what would be his last and most valiant attempt, we can imagine the scene: We see little Joe visibly strain to gather all his strength and power, sucking in the biggest draft of air his little lung sacks could hold. He then pulls himself up on his tippiest tiptoes, arches his back, throws back his head, and, with all his little veins standing out on his little face and neck, yells *"BUTTHOLE!"* with such power as to knock himself flat on his back in the grass where his brother, Paul, lay, laughing hyena-like, tears streaming in helpless hilarity. And that's when they saw their mom behind the screen door. So, that was fun while it lasted.

Many, many, *many* years later, when Paul shared this bit of childhood lore with his friends, everybody nearly wet their pants laughing, and much liquid refreshment was expelled nasally from assorted members of the audience. Everybody agreed that it was one of the funniest things ever in the history of the world—just because of the "stupid-little-boy-stuff" factor. I mean, it's just such a goofy-ass thing to yell—crass enough to be, well, crass, but clearly not on anybody's Top 5 List of Really Bad Words. And so, the Butthole Club was formed, and all present vowed that henceforth and forevermore, whenever they found themselves in a new location, they would christen it with a big *"BUTTHOLE!"* Our friend Rhonda so christened a couple of Alps, even.

I have recommended it to any number of tense and harried individuals who expressed to me a high level of frustration and malevolent feelings toward their spouses, neighbors, and/or fellow employees. I offer it to you now—in all seriousness. The next time you are just *reeeally* pissed off and think you want to commit mayhem—don't Go Postal—Go *Butthole!* Lock yourself in your office or a restroom stall, go off in your car or stand in the middle of a busy street if you're so inclined, and just throw back your head and yell *"BUTTHOLE!"* as loud as you possibly can. Do-overs are certainly allowed if you're not satisfied with your first attempt.

I guarantee you'll feel better *instantly*. If this doesn't dispel your bad mood on the spot—actually, if you don't laugh out loud at the very *thought* of yourself doing this—then I believe you need to seek immediate in-house treatment and a big round of antipsychotics—'cause they be somethin' *bad* wrong with you.

Big Brothers Are Bad News

As we saw in the previous tale, the ever-devious big brother, Paul, led the ever-the-willing-dupe little brother, Joe, astray. It is not reasonable to assume that, left to his own devices, Joe would have ever devised the game of *Butthole* on his own, and even if he had, big brother Paul would never have fallen for it. And you notice Paul was not joining in the Butthole Bellow— this was an omission fraught with malice aforethought. Paul, mistakenly, as it turned out, believed that should a parental unit happen on the scene, Joe would be the only one hollering, and thus he would likewise be the only one hauled off and punished.

And indeed, it might well have played out that way had the game not gone on for so very long—long enough for Mrs. C to hear the sound of a child yelling, identify the word being yelled, realize that the sound was coming from her own front yard, out of the mouth of at least one of her own two children, and get to the front door in time to observe that the yeller had a highly en-thusiastic and very motivating coach exhorting him to try harder.

My daddy was the same kind of bad big brother. He and his baby brother, Bub, were out rambling through the woods of Attala County, Mississippi, one hot summer day when Bub spied some small round brown things on the ground and asked his big brother, John, what they were. Now, if you've ever been around rabbits at all, you already know that their poop looks almost exactly like their food—little pellets. Daddy picked one up and very seriously told Bub this was his lucky day—he had found a stash of "Rabbit Pills," and if he *ate one*, he would catch the next rabbit he saw. And before Daddy could say, "Oh, shit!" Bub had popped one into his little mouth and swallowed it down—excitedly looking around for a rabbit to chase. Before too long, sure enough, a big fat rabbit did cross their path and Bub lit out after that rascal in an astonishing blaze of speed, charged with unshakable faith in the words of his big brother, certain that he would momentarily be clutching to his bosom his very own wild rabbit. Daddy was momentarily hopeful that he might, after all, escape punishment for encouraging his baby brother to eat cottontail caca because Bub did come within a hare's hair of catching the thing. The subsequent wail put up by the empty-handed Bub when the bunny made good his escape could be heard echoing through the woods for miles around, and it wasn't long before Maw came looking—to Daddy—for an explanation—and, as usual, she came armed with a stout switch.

Sex Talk

It's a pretty widely accepted rule, at least in the South, that it's not polite to discuss certain things, like money, religion, or politics. We know better than to talk about those things mostly because we're liable to end up in a fistfight if we do. S-E-X is also on that no-talk list, but, of course, you can't actually *say* that, because, well, that would be acknowledging its existence, and that, as everybody knows, is just the exact same thing as *telling* your teenagers to *have* sex—as soon as possible and with as many partners as they can find, willing or not. If everybody in the world would just refrain from ever talking about S-E-X, I'm sure the teen pregnancy rate would plummet.

In my observation, there is no amount of education, no level of sophistication to which a parent can hope to aspire, that will afford them a sense of comfort and ease when the moment arrives at which the child has deduced that Something Is Definitely Up and sex—easily *the* most complicated issue in the lives of humankind—must somehow be translated into kid-speak and no matter how good a job you *think* you've done— well, just don't count on it is all I'm saying.

You may *think* you've just articulated the whole thing bell-clear and nose-plain—that any first-grader ought to be able to grasp the theory you've just outlined—but you might be surprised what your very own personal first-grader *actually heard* you say. Here are a few totally innocuous misunderstandings— and if these simple messages have been garbled in their little minds, it does not bode well at all for sex education or the catechism.

Queen Kathy's daughter came home from pre-K having learned a song about "where the deer and the cantaloupe play." My own BoPeep once begged me for an hour to sing to her the song about the possums. I turned my feeble brain inside out and back again and could not come up with a single possum-related lyric, yet she insisted that I sang it to her every night— the one about the possums on the vine. The fog lifted and I realized that when I sang to her the love song "Today, while the *blossoms* still cling to the vine," she thought it was a happy little marsupial tune.

Ty reported to his family that his first-grade class was learning about the seasons. His sister asked him what his favorite season was and, Southern to his very core, he replied, "Deer season and turkey season."

Little four-year-old Michael was wearing his parents, his older sister, and everybody in the mall slap *out* with his hollering and whining and begging for everything he saw. He was un-happy because Big Sis Katie was getting new school clothes and the shopping expedition was not, as he felt it should be, enough about *him*. Queen Ellen finally took Katie off in another direction, leaving her husband, Danny, to deal with Sir Mikey. Danny resorted to just hoisting him up and toting him through the stores, but short of putting a bag over the child's head, there was no way to stop him from *seeing* all the merchandise, which translated directly and swiftly into *wanting* all the merchandise. Danny remained calm, and at every plea for every item, he calmly told Michael that, although no purchases would be forthcoming, "Your request has been duly noted," and continued walking. As they were leaving the store and the very last toy was begged for and denied, but "duly noted," Michael pushed back from his dad, looked him square in the eye, and wailed, "But I want it to be *yes-ted!*" Which I actually thought was a pretty good word invention — I'da bought him the dang toy for that one.

Lazy Suzy Bon-Bon was helping her daughter Jill make a T-shirt at Vacation Bible School. It had Jill's little handprints all over it and said, "I am God's handiwork." When Daddy Hal came in that afternoon, Jill couldn't wait to show it off to him, telling him proudly that she was "God's handicap."

Queen Teri's son, Aaron, came racing into the house with the day's mail, jumping back and forth in a good imitation of the pee dance, so excited he couldn't get the words out fast enough, pleading with her, "Mom, we *have* to order this today—*pleeeeze!*" Teri examined the big white envelope that had generated all this excitement with the cover words *"Order now and receive a free afghan!"* "Please order right now, Mama, so we can get the afghan!"

Teri was completely bumfuzzled by his obvious but inexplicable frenzy to avail himself of this amazing free offer as soon as possible and she asked him exactly what his plans were for this free afghan. The answer came in that tone of voice that lets a parent know just *how* stupid they think you are. *"Du-u-u-h!* Teach him to speak *English!*"

We can only imagine Aaron's crushing disappointment when he learned it was not exactly an exciting, new sort of immigration program but just a free blanket.

Religion is just about as tricky a subject as sex, I reckon. My daddy never got tired of the jokes that grew out of the childish malapropisms from my seester, Judy's, and my childhood Christmases. We once made a drawing of the Nativity scene featuring all the usual cast of characters, human, animal, and heavenly, but in one bottom corner of the picture was a very short, very fat man that Daddy could not place in his recollection of the Christmas story. With, I'm sure, the eye-roll and the du-u-u-uh tone, he was advised that it was a picture of the song "Silent Night"—as if that should make all things clear to him, but it didn't. Another dose of eye-rolling accompanied the answer "That's Round John Virgin!"

When we were children—and still to this day—the most exciting point of the holiday season for Judy and me is the day before Christmas—because *that* marks the arrival of "Christmas *Steve*." Daddy thought "Christmas Steve" was the funniest thing he ever heard in his whole life, I think—we got a lot of mileage out of that one. And of course, Easter brought not only the Bunny but, more important, that most High Holy Event— "Erection Sunday."

Daddy never grew tired of recalling the little girl in the very fancy and, of course, *new* Easter dress who had been politely receiving compliments all morning, but for some reason, when the Preacher's attention was directed her way, she felt that a more pithy response was called for—one that would demonstrate her appreciation, not only for the compliment but for the dress itself and for the sacrifices that were made in order that she might shine so radiantly on this special day. "Thank you so much! But my mama says it is a *bitch* to iron."

On the way to church one Sunday morning, Queen Kaye decided it was as good a time as any to take her daughter with her to Big People's Church, and so she began, in the car, to explain to her little girl the whole concept and tradition of Holy Communion. The miles just flew by as Kaye's long-winded explanation wore on. "The first thing you'll see is the Preacher will come out . . ." and she detailed all the different things the Preacher would say and how then the Preacher would do thus and so and so forth and so on. And the little angel just sat quietly, seeming to understand every word—at least it seemed so to Kaye. In truth, I think the child was just intent on admiring her new white patent leather shoes and frilly socks—because as her mama finally wrapped up this highway catechism class she asked if her darling had any questions. And the little girl very excitedly asked, "What does the Creature *look like,* Mommy?"

BoPeep's buddy Kate loved to say grace at every meal, but instead of the traditional Christian closing, "In Christ's name, Amen," Kate would conclude with "Come on in, old man," but I always figgered God was happy enough just to get the call—I don't imagine He stands on ceremony too strong where little folks are concerned.

But, then, sometimes it seems they *do* get it—like when Ty learned all the words to "Jesus Loves the Little Children" and he couldn't get enough of singing it and talking about it. He told his mama that Jesus really did love all the little children and Mama, of course, readily agreed. He then added that he also believed that Jesus loves all the parents, too—even those like her.

Many a parent's been asked by a child questions regarding mysteries about God that have baffled the human race since its invention. Case in point: Sarajean and her son Mike were engaged in a most serious discussion about God and the origin of Life. "God made everything, right?" he asked. "And everybody, too?" "Yes," Sarajean replied, "God made the whole world and everybody in it." "Did God make Mallory, too?" Sarajean assured him that, yes, God even made the second-grade class bully, a particularly mean little girl named Mallory. *"Why?"* was Mike's follow-up question, to which Sarajean admits she had no immediate response.

Tess's little brother was a shithead—and there is written proof of this—written in his own hand, no less. Bro was bad to act up in church and was constantly in need of reprimanding, which he got. So fine: One day, Mom was home, doing Mom Stuff, minding her own business, when she received a phone call from an elder in the church. Mom was a bit surprised to receive the call—couldn't imagine its purpose—and the longer the conversation went on, the less enlightened she became. The caller was telling her how the Church "was there for her" and how everyone knew how "stressful it is to be a Mother" and that she could and should "always lean on the Church for support."

Mom was thinking this was just *such* a sweet call until the caller was winding down and informed Mom that "her prayer request had been received" and that the congregation would certainly be praying for her in church that very evening. Whoa, whoa, whoa! Mom hadn't *filled out* any prayer request cards. Caller advised her that the card with her name on it was in the church office—and that it bore a prayer request for "anger management problems—especially with my son."

Caller and Mom had a big laugh—Mom still has the prayer request card to this very day—and Bro is still a shithead, according to Tess.

The point of all this is that the older your child gets, the less margin you have for error when it comes to S-E-X and the way that he or she *thinks* it works. There's time for study and reflection and soul-searching where religion is concerned, but S-E-X has been cut-and-dried for a good many centuries and everybody needs to know what goes where and why.

Queen Beth works for a pediatric dentist. A little boy once told her, very somberly, that he was getting glasses and he knew why. The reason *she* erroneously assumed he was getting glasses was that he was either nearsighted or farsighted, but he quickly informed her of the real—top-secret—reason he was getting glasses. In a graveyard whisper, he confessed that his dad had left his glasses on the bathroom sink and that he had surreptitiously tried them on—and in so doing, he had caught his daddy's germs and now *he* needed glasses, too. I can only hope these parents did a better job of explaining sex than they did optometry.

What kids don't know *can* hurt them, it can result in more *of* them, and, yes, it can even kill them.

We need to make absolutely certain that they really do understand what goes where and why—and also why *not*. And then check and double-check that what you *said* is what they *heard*. After all, the Message Received *is* The Message—so be sure to check out the reception.

In the spirit of full disclosure, Queen Regina shared with her three-year-old son that she wouldn't be able to pick him up from preschool the next day, and she gave him a little info about a surgical procedure she was having performed. Very matter-of-fact and mature. Only he went to school the next day and told the teacher, "My mom doesn't feel good. She got her boobs tied yesterday."

Parents who have already survived their children's teenage years should fall to their knees, weeping tears of joyous gratitude that they are not being called upon to deal with what is truly a whole new world, sexually speaking. Parents who still have this ahead of them—we will just put y'all in the prayer box. I don't know of anything else we can do for you, bless your hearts.

Things are different out there today, and from where I'm sitting, it is looking like a *bonanza* for boys. Since penises were invented, surely this is the best time in history to have one. According to most experts and teens alike, oral sex is *the* thing—and brace yourselves—it's often done in groups or with multiple partners. (I'm about to throw up just writing that about a group of people, many of whom are not even old enough to drive, let alone vote.)

Young girls today are much more aggressive—very often

the initiators of sex of any kind—almost a complete role reversal, if you will. *But,* believe it or not, guys (of all ages) are not as completely thrilled with this as we might expect—which may (we can all hope) actually end up having a *positive* effect on the alarming teen pregnancy rate. Some scientific-types did a study, using the ubiquitous white rats, and found that when the normal ratty "courtship" rituals were prevented between the males and females, the birth rate went down significantly. If the rat version of the mating dance that they are hardwired to do doesn't get done, nothing much else gets done either.

I've spoken with any number of guys—ranging in age from around fifteen to around seventy—and not a one of them is anywhere near as ecstatic over the current overstock situation in the blow job department as I would have guessed. Most of them really do still want to "chase the car" for a bit. They still *reeeeally* want to catch it, but just not on the first block.

Of course, there are always exceptions.

I have a couple of friends who have a thirteen-year-old son. We'll call the wife "Tammy," the husband "Bob," and the son "Juniorbob," just so the Juniorbob doesn't murder Tammy in her sleep for telling me this.

From the time Juniorbob was very young, Tammy and Bob had determined to be very open and frank in discussing sex with him, and they frequently congratulated themselves on the very excellent lines of communication they felt they had developed over the years.

Okay, so now that Juniorbob was taking seventh-grade health, Tammy had just read all manner of material regarding the current trend toward female sexual aggression, and she trembled for her little baby Juniorbob and his delicate psyche. She was also not a little concerned about the real dangers that he could encounter, so she thought this was a perfect time to bring up the subjects of STDs, aggressive girls, and oral sex. Turns out Juniorbob was unaware that a person could get HIV from oral sex since it's not transmitted through saliva. Tammy asked him if he'd ever bitten his tongue or cheek or if he ever saw any blood when he brushed his teeth.

Bob was there for this little gabfest but he didn't contribute much beyond his presence. Tammy did most of the talking, and after the STD thing, she went on and talked to her son about what to do if a girl wanted to kiss him or go further, and he, for whatever reason, felt uncomfortable, and on and on and blah blah blah with all manner of really excellent but nonetheless *parental* advice—which, of course, is automatically suspect even if it's as obvious as "stick your head under the faucet, your hair is on fire."

Tammy was feeling quite the Good Parent for imparting such wisdom and sage advice to her young son, but she noted that he was wearing a somewhat perplexed look on his face, so she asked him if he had any questions for her or his father. Juniorbob looked them dead square in the eye and asked, in all earnestness, "You don't really expect me to turn down a blow job, do you?" Tammy and Bob fell to the floor laughing, and when they could finally get their breath, Tammy hoisted herself up and said, "Talk to your father," and walked out. Said she didn't even want to *know* what the answer was—there's a limit to just how much enlightenment we can stand.

It's also good to let our children know that—as even the best-intentioned parents—we *do* sometimes make mistakes ourvery-ownselves—sometimes what we're thinking in our heads comes out of our mouths in the very wrongest way—sometimes we, too, make asses of ourselves—and this knowledge can be of comfort to them. Queen Bess recalled her own dread before her first visit to the gynecologist—we can all pretty much relate. When it became first-visit time for her daughters, she empathized with their discomfort, and to shore up their composure, she shared with them her own personal moment of utmost embarrassment—thinking that they would relax and feel fairly bulletproof— because no matter what—*nothing* could be as bad as *that*.

Young Bess's Shining Moment had come after she had been suffering—and I do mean s-u-f-f-e-r-i-n-g—with a raging yeast infection, and this was in the dark days before you could buy Monistat over the counter. She was ready to hump a hedgehog just to get some relief from the itch by the time she finally got in to see the doctor. As it happened, this was her first visit to this particular physician, so she was probably a little nervous, which would surely account for her unfortunate choice of words when, in the stirrups, with the doc and the nurse down there under the sheet, she was attempting to convey to them just how very miserable this condition had indeed rendered her. "I swear, I am going to lose my mind if I don't get this thing licked." Bess was *meaning,* of course, that she reeeally wanted to get this little health problem solved, but *saying* something else entirely.

I imagine having this benchmark for self-humiliation will serve Bess's daughters well in many areas of their lives.

Of course, no matter how good a job you do interpreting the Birds and the Bees to your child, he or she will not ever really believe that either one of you has ever actually *been* a "bird" or a "bee." And it is a fact that after your children make their much-heralded appearance in your life, there is usually a correlative dip in the activity of the birds and the bees in your home. Sigh.

Queen Ade was helping her seven-year-old daughter get ready for bed and the child said, "You know how women have hair—down there? Well, I was wondering, do boys have hair, too?" Ade confirmed that, yes, boys have hair down there, too, and asked Baby Girl why she hadn't asked before, if she'd been curious. Baby Girl looked surprised and said, "I didn't think you'd *know*! How *do* you know?" She sounded really quite shocked by this development. Ade, having been caught unprepared with a lie like "read it in a book" or "somebody told me" or "saw a picture," just confessed that she had, in fact, seen a boy naked. Baby Girl was clearly astonished at this revelation and she gasped, "Was it Daddy?"

At least Baby Girl was willing to allow for the possibility of a possibility where her parents were concerned. Kate's daughter was not quite so open-minded. When she was about eight, little Ellen boasted that she "knew what sex was." Kate naturally made a few inquiries to determine the exact level of knowledge acquired by Ellen from sources unknown, although the older brother was a good bet for the most likely suspect.

Ellen said it was when two people got in bed without their clothes on—which was more accuracy than Kate would have expected from the brother. Ellen went on to add that she "knew for a fact that you and Dad have not had sex since I have been born" (which Kate also noted for near-perfect accuracy). Kate, stifling a snort, asked her why she thought that and Ellen said, "Because every time I come into your bedroom, you both always have your clothes on." Kate was content to let that one stand.

Queen Sarah has about a thousand kids, give or take, and three of 'em are triplets that came along a good while after anybody would have reasonably anticipated such a thing. Nobody was more surprised than Sarah and her hubby, let me tell you, but they just kept perking right along where lesser individuals might have caused great physical harm to themselves or each other. We salute them—we practically bow down to them when we hear that, when the triplets were ten years old, there is a story involving Sarah and her husband *and* S-E-X. I mean, really, nobody would fault a couple of semi-old gee's if they never did it again after triplets, now, would they? It perks me up no end to hear about this—makes me want to step up my own level of participation, seeing as how I only ever had the *one* little ole girl-baby and The Cutest Boy in the World never had any babies of *any* kind. If Sarah and her man are still at it with ten-year-old triplets (*boys*, no less—besides all them other kids), me and Kyle have practically a moral *obligation* to be getting after it night and day. This strikes me as a most excellent idea with which Kyle is certain to concur.

Anyway, Mr. Sarah was headed out of town to care for his sick daddy and Sarah didn't want to send him off "pent up," so she thought she'd best do a little preemptive damage control with the rank and file still residing in the homeplace—all of which were assembled in Sis's room for some inexplicable reason, since there was not usually much fraternization among the boys and their sister.

So, Sarah popped in on them and told them that if they needed or anticipated developing a need for anything located in her bedroom, bathroom, closet, or medicine cabinet, they should go and get it forthwith. The Quiet Son looked at her and asked, "Mom, are you going to lock the door?" Sarah, feeling trapped in an unwelcome spotlight of her own creation, swallowed hard and said, "Yes."

Whereupon a knowing and gleeful grin grew on Sonnyboy's face and soon spread to his brothers and sister. "*We* know what *y'all* are going to be doing!" he said with the air of a sage, and they all nodded in pleased agreement. Sarah choked and mustered a pretty weak "What's that, honey?" A unified shout went up from the troops as Sonnyboy shouted, *"You're going to wrap our Christmas presents!"*

With a completely straight face, Sarah backed out of the room, congratulating herself inwardly for producing such a fine crop of greedy—but still innocent—chirren.

One of our very fine SPQ Wannabe™ chapters in Oklahoma is proud to be herded around by the very capable BossQueen Stephanie. Close friends for years, the group originally came together for their Young Couples Bible Study, but since they are Episcopalians, this was actually *fun*. Over many bottles of wine, the men carried on about sports and assorted manly pursuits of no interest to normal people while elsewhere on the premises, over many more bottles of wine, the women commiserated about raising kids and putting up with husbands—in particular, the never-particularly-well-timed sexual desires and advances of said husbands.

Stephanie said that what she thought they all needed could be found in *National Lampoon's Vacation*—when John Candy stands at the foot of the bed and says, "Sorry, folks—park's closed—moose out front shoulda told ya!" And thus, they came up with their very own set of Rules for Governing Sex after Children:

1. The Park is open only when the "Park Manager" (read: wife) gives the All Clear. The All Clear means that all Attractions are up to standard—it does not guarantee that all are, in fact, open. Some Attractions are not and never will be available. (Author's addendum: If any Campers are disgruntled over this ruling, they should perhaps consider exploring their own Attractions.)

2. The Attractions have rules. No one may ride unless certain specifications are met. All specifications are set at the total discretion of the Park Manager and are subject to change without notice. Depending on the mood of the Park Manager, some Attractions may be Shows Only, while others may be more interactive and participatory in nature.

3. Personal Park Hopper Passes are available but Campers should expect to pay hefty Fees (covering the cost of paying someone to take care of the children for a week while all the Park Managers go off on a va-*∂amn*-cation that includes but is not restricted to shopping, drinking, shopping, lolling in the sun, drinking, and, of course, shopping—funds for all of which will also be included in the Fees). Only when the Fees are paid in full will the Personal Park Hopper Pass be valid, and it, like so many things in this life, has an expiration date.

4. *Positively NO Early Admission to the Park.* All Attractions must be readied before the first guest enters. This re-

quires some pre-Attraction setup, preview, and the occasional practice run of some sort. The Park Manager will not give the All Clear to open the Park if the rides' wheels have not been properly lubed.

5. The Park is subject to closing for repairs—either major (plastic surgery) or minor (eating the whole damn cake because it was easier than putting it away).

Over time, Steph tells me, the husbands familiarized themselves with the Park, came to understand its inner workings, and the Park Managers have never tired of their jobs. The rules can actually be distilled as follows: Camper Does Right—Park's Open!; Camper Does Bad—Park Is Closed; Camper Screws Around—Park Is Relocating.

I do kinda like thinking of myself as Disney World, don't you?

Sometimes the Universe Just Sends You the Message That You Are Not Taking Enough Time for Yourself These Days.

Queen Kaye suspected that she was losing her mind chasing after four kids, and when she found herself at a gathering where there were several other folks who were sharing a similar heaping portion from Nature's Bounty, she was most anxious to make their acquaintance to see if she could garner any helpful hints for herding her horde of hairy hounds from hell.

Toward the end of the evening she found herself in conversation with a fairly frazzled looking father of four, and they commenced the commiseration when she allowed as how she and her husband had also been quadruply honored by the stork. "How nice," he said, probably not very sincerely. "What are their ages?" "We've got a thirteen-year-old, a nine-year-old, a four-year-old, and one that's three," she wearily replied. "And how about the sex?" he asked politely. This struck her as an odd question, clearly indicating that she was in *bad* need of about a dozen different kinds of R&R, but for the sake of honest and forthright discussion, she said, "Well, actually, it's not bad—thanks for asking." Realizing, of course, as *soon* as the last consonant rolled off her tongue, that he had actually been inquiring as to the various genders of her offspring. Clearly, she has *got* to get out of that house without those kids a little more.

Granted, married folks have a hard time getting any once the tiny feet pitter-pattering in the halls start coming in sets of two instead of four. I swear, you could have forty-five dogs to take care of and you'd still have ample time for a roll in your sweet baby's arms—but bring just one actual infant home and you barely have the time, energy, or inclination to roll your eyes at each other or replace the roll of toilet paper—romantic rolling is rarely on the agenda.

But *single* parents—that would be single *custodial* parents, of course—we're talking serious adult sensory deprivation here—any adult thought, feeling, or activity that does not directly relate to the care and feeding of minor children is shelved in favor of something to do with the minor children. Having been one myownself for many years, I know full well how the single parent is constantly tried and tribulated — bless their little hearts and their nether regions, too — 'cause neither area gets too much outside attention, and, frankly, time for self-love is pretty limited, too.

Nobody on this earth has worked or ever will work as hard as a full-time mom or dad with an additional full-time job outside the home. And again I say it — it cannot be said too much or even enough — bless their little hearts.

And when they do make the absolutely herculean effort required to carve out some tiny bit of life for themselves (i.e., find a roll-around partner), they are quite often met with somewhat less than rousing support from the kids' quarters. Queen Candace was getting dressed for a very rare "hot date," and she had really put on the full-court press in her preparations. She had done her hair, she had artfully applied a whole faceful of makeup, and she was wearing what she imagined to be a really cute outfit. Her ten-year-old daughter came into the bathroom/dressing area to check the progress of the transformation from Mom to Woman with a Date. She took her time with her assessment, and finally made the proclamation that Candace was hoping for: "Mom, you look *really hot.*" Candace was flushed with smug pleasure and said, "Why, thank you, sweetie." To which Sweetie responded, "No, I mean sweaty."

I'm sure Candace went straight and wrote that down in Sweetie's baby book—and I bet she bore down pretty good when she was writing it, too.

Queen Kara's little angel was delighted with her new toy— a wand, purported to be magic—and she was anxious to test its powers. Angel magnanimously offered to grant any wish Kara desired, and Kara said, "Make me beautiful." Indicating an affirmative response, Angel obligingly passed the wand over Kara, making the appropriate magic wand sound as she did. Pause. Another waving of the wand. And another. Finally, banging it on the table and positively spewing frustration, Angel sputtered, "Dang thing's not working!"

Parenting of any variety but particularly the single kind can not only rob us of any shred of sense of our own formerly at least simmering, if not scorching hot, perception of ourselves as sexual beings, but it's usually a job pretty much devoid of anything like "thanks," too—at least until the children grow up, reproduce, and then *really* grow up. Until that day, they really have no concept at all of things like "Where do clean clothes come from?" and "When do moms sleep?" Do da words "payback time" mean anythin' to ya? But that's some long years, waiting for all that stuff that went around to come on back around, and it can be a lonely time, waiting for the little buggers to leave the nest and encounter enough Real Life to fully appreciate the multitude of sacrifices that were made on their behalf.

I personally have taken a solemn vow that should my daughter Bailey ever present me with grandchildren, I will quit work and borrow money if I have to in order to have sufficient time and funds with which to spoil those kids irreversibly rotten. Makes me giggle with anticipation.

Stranger Danger

No children were harmed in the writing of this chapter — but several did receive some pretty serious threats, and their ongoing Security Level has been raised to Orange.

More than anything, including air, parents want to protect their children from any and all harm. We survey our homes for potential hazards and take appropriate measures to secure the premises. There are covers and locks on everything that could be fallen into or mistakenly opened by a little person. No knicks or knacks are in sight, and nearly all our possessions are on shelves so high that we ourownselves can't reach 'em. When we want to take a pill, we often have to smash the bottle open with a hammer — so "childproof" are the caps — but hammers are too dangerous to have around. Neither we nor our clothes are particularly clean because the hot-water heater has been set at "tepid." We have to go out to bars to drink — there is no alcohol, rubbing or otherwise. Forks and knives are considered too dangerous, we eat everything with spoons, and there's not a toothpick within a hundred yards of us. No matches, no lighters — open flames are not permitted. All pieces of heavy furniture have been bolted to the wall to prevent toppling in the event the furniture does double duty as a climbing wall. We can watch only *Muffy Mouse* or *Sesame Street* on TV — everything else is under "parental control" lockdown and we can't remember how to unlock it. Stairways are blocked by "safety" gates — the locking mechanisms of which would challenge the skills of a Ph.D. in Theoretical Condensed Matter Physics from Oxford University — which we are not — so we risk limbs and lives climbing over them.

And so on and so forth — the point obviously being that we go to great lengths in our attempts to make our living spaces childproof to secure the safety of our precious children. (Although it's shocking to me how many parents will not leave a bucket of mop water unattended but, tragically, loaded pistols are often too easily accessible.) We also counsel them on as many worst-case scenarios as we can without making them too terrified to leave their rooms. Although when you read this next part, you might think it a good plan for these kids to remain in their rooms indefinitely.

The Stranger Danger Strategies taught by everybody from Winnie the Pooh to Dr. Phil have apparently been honed into very fine weapons by an alarming segment of the butthead child population. Yes. I received not one or two but a whole big *bunch* of reports from highly disgruntled parents who had narrowly avoided being perp-walked out of any number of shopping malls and grocery stores where they had quite properly attempted to remove their very own personal butthead children who were loudly and with great animation doing their utmost to live up to that description—in order that they (the highly disgruntled parents) might seek to more privately reason with them (the butthead children) about this totally unacceptable behavior being performed in this very public place. The buttheads may have inferred that they were in some sort of immediate physical danger. Being buttheaded does not in anyway hinder innate intelligence, and the children were no doubt picking up on the subtle body-language cues from the disgruntled parents—bulging veins in the forehead, squinty eyes, guttural speaking tone, clenched teeth, throbbing muscles in the jaw, and/or flying specks of spittle. The rare parent is able, in situations provoking intense disgruntlement, to produce actual live steam and project it from his or her ear holes. When this happens, even the most dedicated butthead becomes aware that his/her Security Level has just leaped above the Red Zone and that if there is a fan anywhere in the vicinity, it will presently be slinging shit and he/she is going to be the primary target.

The butthead quickly surveys the disgruntled parent and

the disapproving faces in the crowd along with his/her own likelihood of coming out of this altercation unscathed, and mentally acknowledges that the odds are not looking too good. Survival instincts kick in and the little butthead is suddenly no longer pitching a full-blown hissy fit in the middle of the Kroger brought on by the parent's unreasonable refusal to permit the opening and on-site consumption of a twelve-pound bag of Gummy Bears thirty minutes before suppertime. The butthead has smoothly—imperceptibly—shifted gears. He/she is still yelling, all right—loud enough to startle even the deafest seventy-five-year-old security guard and bring him running to the aid of the butthead, who is alerting *everybody in the store* that there is a child abduction under way right before their very eyes in the neighborhood grocery store where they shop every week and they always thought it was so safe and nothing like that ever happens here—and yet—here it is, happening.

The butthead has commenced writhing in the arms of the disgruntled parent and screaming, *"No, I won't go! You're not my mommy!* [or *Daddy,* as the case may be.] *Let me go! Help! Help!"* And suddenly the crowd that was so disapproving of the little butthead only scant moments ago is now galvanized on his/her behalf and the disgruntled parent is surrounded by vigilante grocery shoppers, the doors are locked, and the actual police sirens can already be heard approaching as the cops arrive to thwart the snatching of this child.

It takes a fair amount of time to convince the police and the bloodthirsty crowd that this butthead does, in fact, belong to and with this disgruntled parent and the child was not being so much just "snatched" as he/she was about to be "snatched bald-headed," as we say in the South. (It means that the child was about to be quite sternly reprimanded.)

Sorry to report that I have no preventive measures to offer regarding this potentiality—other than the obvious *Peter and the Wolf* analogy—but I did feel strongly that you, as parents or potential parents or friends of parents, had a right to and, indeed, a need for at least a warning. Your awareness and preparedness for this type of occurrence should be especially heightened if your butthead children are either adopted or happen to look more like the other parent. Carrying photo IDs of such children would not, in my opinion, be an unnecessarily excessive precaution. You do not want to be put in jail for even a few hours on a charge of kidnapping—even if it is a gross error caused by the überbuttheadedness of your own kid. People who do bad things to children do not fare well in jail—and I personally have no problem with that at all—so you will want to take preemptive steps to avoid this at all costs.

Some folks will never be at risk for mistaken identity in relation to their offspring—the family resemblance is so strong as to support the belief that human cloning has been successfully conducted for decades. I could be in downtown Hong Kong in rush-hour traffic and spot a "Molpus" or a "Puckett" relative at a hundred yards.

She Doesn't Look Familiar but I'd Know
That Voice Anywhere!

Queen Cassie of the Debutantes of Dubious Distinction is the delightedly devoted mama of Brianna, who apparently makes Shirley Temple seem homely and dull. Cassie was a city girl who married Grizzly Adams (not his real name) and went off with him to do some happily-ever-aftering in an East Texas town where a 4-H fund-raiser is the hot social ticket.

Cassie and Grizzly decided to adopt a child, and after researching a number of agencies, settled on one in China, and off they went for a couple of weeks to an unpronounceable province, joyously returning home with their beautiful baby girl, who became an instant local celebrity. Cassie found her own status immediately improved as well. Overnight, she miraculously went from being "that ole city gal Grizzly Adams married" to "little Brianna's Mommy," in most but not quite *all* the locals' minds and conversations.

One of Grizzly's lifelong buddies was visiting with Grizzly's elderly aunt, and the lady remarked, "That shore is a purty baby Grizzly and his wife had, but she don't look nuthin' like her daddy." The buddy chuckled and said, "Oh, no, ma'am, Grizzly and Cassie adopted that baby—they went all the way to China to get her." Auntie was having none of it. "*Chiner?* I ain't never heard of nobody goin' all the way to *Chiner* to adopt no baby. If y'ask me, that's just a story been concocted to pull the wool over ever'body's eyes. You know that ole gal Grizzly married is from *Houston,* and you *know* how fast them Houston wimmin are."

The question was also raised as to whether or not little Brianna would have an "accent." Smart-ass Cassie said, oh, yeah, that was a given—thinking to herself, "Just not a *Chinese* one." Cassie says Brianna already sounds like a natural-born East Texan. As her proud daddy was holding her while strolling around the backyard, Brianna pointed at the ground and yelled excitedly, "Looky thar, Deddy—*far ain'ts!*" Translation: Oh, look, Daddy—fire ants!

Discipline, Values, and Remaining Unincarcerated

If You Can Teach Them Only One Thing

A nd most of us consider ourselves to be fortunate geniuses if we are able at some point in our parental careers to demonstrate that we have managed to teach them even *one* thing—so if they get nothing else from you but the following, you can rest on at least one fair-sized laurel. I am still of the opinion that the admonition we received from our Granddaddy Harvey was the best, if not the *only,* advice needed to equip one to successfully navigate life itsownself—*"BE PARTICULAR"* does pretty much cover every situation and potentiality. There is *no* time when this does not apply, *no* scenario not improved by its application. I offer it to you, yet again. (See also my first book, *The Sweet Potato Queen's Book of Love* — and all the rest of 'em, too. I *really* want you to *be particular.*)

If, by chance, you are afforded the opportunity to impart any *other* bits of wisdom to your children, then take a stab at tolerance. (Sorry about that unfortunate choice of words there.) I have always tried to teach my daughter that it's best to hate people on an individual basis only. Yes, this *is* more time-consuming and labor-intensive, but I do find it serves us all best if we gather our own information about another person before we choose to despise them. It does fall under the broad umbrella dome of Being Particular — and, by the way, it should apply to loving them as well. Yes, it is fine to "love" them in a generic, global, fellow-human kind of way without having any personal contact — but if we're going to bring them *home* to "love," we need to be particular about that personal profile.

Queen Denise says that her children are all very bright — at least they do personally believe that they know *everything* — and she has always tried to teach them to "respect everyone," and in instances where they encountered persons not exactly respect-worthy, she's attempted to teach them to "fake it." That could certainly come in handy in the corporate world.

Of course, as a confirmed *smoker,* Denise does create somewhat of an uphill battle for herself when it comes to trying to teach her kids to *not* do things that are, oh, say, *deadly.* In this case, they are the ones lecturing and nagging *her* for endangering not only her own health but *theirs* as well. And to that she replied, with a big puff of smoke, "That may well be—but some days, this cigarette's the only thing keeping y'all alive." They had no snappy rejoinder for that one.

If I Could Rest My Eyes for a Minute or Two

I recently spoke at a fund-raiser in Pendleton, Oregon, for the Pioneer Relief Nursery—talk about an idea whose time has come. This organization does just what the name implies—it provides child care to give *relief*—blessed, rare-as-the-unicorn relief—for families considered to be "at risk for abuse." Hunny, let me tell you what—that group is any and *all* families that include children of any sort. There has never breathed a parent who didn't come close enough to at least *see* that Line—and any claiming otherwise are liars—and, of course, fools if they think anybody believes it. Yes, thankfully, *most* back away from that Line—in horror and terror at how close they could have been to crossing that Line—but all have at least seen it.

Because there just *are* those days when everything that can will go wrong and your nerves are either the fraying rope supporting you over the bottomless abyss or they are the sputtering fuse coming ever closer to the keg of dynamite—or perhaps yours are more like the agonizing fingertips clutching desperately to the ledge and your children are the ones stomping on those cramping digits. Pick your poison—everybody has Those Days sooner or later. Wouldn't it be fantastic if there was a Relief Nursery in every neighborhood with a drive-thru where you could just wheel up and shove your kids out your window and into theirs—out of your hands, twitching with the overpowering desire to strangle, and into the gentle hands of a sweet and infinitely patient person—just for a little while—just long enough for you to locate that sweet and infinitely patient person you used to be—the one you were BEFORE you had these irritating children.

I have met *sooooo many* incredibly gifted, wise, and long-suffering parents who have never been actually tested and tried (not to mention found wanting and convicted) by the little infinitesimal detail of having gone through the whole deal of, you know, being pregnant, giving birth—or adopting—and then trying to domesticate any little wild animals of their *own*. Neither their boundless theories nor their time, wallets, and psyches have ever been subjected to any sort of scientific study for determining proof—on account of they ain't never had them no kids in they own houses to fool with.

As a matter of fact, this phenomenon also exists to a very large degree amongst people *with* children—as regards the always-inferior Children of Others. I myownself could raise *other people's children* quickly, painlessly—*in my sleep, even*—so very clear to me it is, all the stuff those parents are doing wrong and how simple the remedy would be. I marvel that they cannot seem to see it for themselves when there it is, just as obvious as socks on a rooster.

Whenever a child is in some manner not living above and beyond the expectations of any outside observer, a ration of blame equal to or greater than the transgression of the child will be promptly dumped upon the heads and doorstep of the parents, with the lion's share accruing to the mother of said child. Simultaneous with the blame delivery, a blatantly obvious, embarrassingly simple solution to the situation will also pop, unbidden, into the mind of the outside observer.

This is because raising the children of other people is just *the* easiest thing imaginable—anybody can do it, with no tools, no textbooks—not even an actual introduction to the kids in question is required, come to think of it.

The only thing that complicates and raises immeasurably the degree of difficulty in child rearing is when they send you home with one or more of your *own* to deal with. It's unbelievable, really, how much more demanding, difficult, draining, and downright undignified everything is when it involves you interacting with your own children.

Fear the Fate Factor

None of the theories you have regarding the Children of Others will work when applied to your own children—or, if they do, it's pure blind luck. The absolute worst thing you can ever do as a parent is to start patting yourself on the back for doing such a great job with this kid. When things are, for whatever reason, going well with family, your main goal should be to try to remain under Fate's radar.

To your child, of course, the heavens should reverberate with your loudly sung praises for each and every accomplishment. There is no suggested limit on the level of pride and delight you should express about them to them. Fate knows that we adore our children, approves of it, and thus pays no mind to this sort of thing.

Where Fate is lying in wait for us is when we speak to other parents about the perfection of our children. Hard to tell which upsets Fate more, bragging about our own kids or making snide and superior remarks about other people's. Either way, you are begging for a smack-down of the severest order.

If your kid is making straight As, building Habitat houses, and giving blood every three weeks and your neighbor complains that his kid is failing spelling, vandalizing schools, and selling plasma to buy meth—the only way to placate Fate is to tsk, tsk with your neighbor about These Kids Nowadays and mumble something encouraging to him about spell-check changing the world, admire the superb style of his kid's graffiti, and say that at least he was earning his own drug money and not stealing, like so many others.

If he should call attention to your child's near-angelic status, you must appear to downplay it somewhat—perhaps even hinting that there are probably all manner of crimes and misdemeanors you just haven't uncovered yet. Or you could intimate that, oh, sure, things are great *now*—but, whooboy, you should have seen what we went through when he/she was five—anything to throw Fate off your scent. And *run away as fast as you can* before you are tempted to brag, bellow, and/or bugle about your own unbelievable good fortune—coupled, of course, with pride in your own obviously brilliant parenting skills—to have produced this absolutely stellar human being in the person of your own beloved child. Go home—brag, bellow, and bugle all you want to family members—or even to other friends who are *not* currently enduring hell at the hands of their offspring.

If you are momentarily enjoying a relatively angst-free time as a parent, you should take vacation time from work and spend it *on your knees*, in constant prayers of praise and thanksgiving. And you don't have to worry about using up all your vacation time with this—on account of, as a parent, angst-free time hardly *ever* happens. Even if your kids are models of exemplary behavior, you worry that they'll fall in with a bad crowd—or be in the wrong place at the wrong time—or they'll get sick. If worry burned calories, there would be no fat parents, that's for sure. Parental angst is pervasive and perennial.

Okay, but other than constant pleas to the Almighty for guidance and protection, there are a few methods and theories you can at least *attempt* in your quest to one day present to the world a semiresponsible, sort-of self-reliant, nearly fully functioning human being.

A Little Fear Is Fine, Frankly

Queen Margaret is a wily one, she is. The parent of a teenager quickly learns that once you impose a curfew, the burden of enforcing it falls heavily upon your own tired shoulders. This means you have to work all day, then sit up half the night, watching the clock until curfew time—with your heart only half beating, your lungs only half filling—until the awaited one either arrives and restores your regular rhythms or *doesn't* and all respiration activity in the parent ceases. Parenting is a helluva job, I keep telling you.

Well, after too many sleep-starved weekend nights, our Margaret found a stone that slays many feathered creatures: She just goes and gets into her teenage son's *bed* and goes to *sleep*. The first time he came creeping into the house—late—and tippy-tippy-tip-toed down the hall and creepy-like-a-little-mouse slid into his bed and was juuuust about to breathe a barely audible sigh of relief at having made it in undetected—Margaret—undetected herownself on the other side of the bed—spoke to him from the darkness, inquiring whether or not he had any *idea what time it was.*

He nearly had to change the sheets, she scared him so bad.

And the whole *ICK* factor of thinking oneself to be such a Big Dog, coming in from a Big Night on the Town and finding *your mother* in your bed—*EWWWWW*—well, it was simply not to be borne. It was enough to create in him a healthy embrace of the decreed curfew hour from that day forward, and Margaret suffers only the most minor sleep interruption as she moves from his bed to her own—where she then blissfully rests with the knowledge that her baby bird is safe in the nest once more.

Peggy's widowed brother, Pete, was having a few "issues" with his teenage son David, and he called on Peggy to ask how she had handled certain situations with her now-successfully-grown-up son, Ed. Peggy talked to Pete for a very long time, and when she was done offering what she considered to be sage advice and wisdom born of her vast experience, Pete totally blew her off, told her she was *lucky* Ed had turned out so well, but it sure wasn't anything *she* had done.

Her curiosity piqued by Pete's put-down, she asked Ed why *he* thought he turned out so well—*was* it just "luck" or had her guidance and teachings played a part? He looked her square in the eye and, with nary a glimmer of a grin, said, "I always knew you had a gun."

To this day, Peggy has no idea if he was serious or teasing—nor does she *care*. Something worked—whether she was conscious of it or not—she's just appropriately grateful.

I, myownself, have never been a proponent of corporal punishment. This is yet another one of those things—like sharing stuff and crying yourself to sleep alone—that do not exist as acceptable occurrences in the world of adults. Adults don't willingly share, they rarely gut through any problem alone when they can enlist the aid of friends, family, and/or highly paid therapists, and if they hit each other, one of them ends up in the hoosegow.

And *NO*, hitting your kids is *not* justified in the Bible. "Spare the rod and spoil the child" *does not appear in the Bible.* The verse, bastardized by bastards who want to beatify beating their babies, is actually *Proverbs* 13:24, and it says, "He who spares the rod hates his son but he who loves him is diligent to discipline him."

The point being that parents should discipline their children—meaning *guide and direct them*—it does *not* mean to hit them. The "rod" in the Bible was used by shepherds to defend and guide the sheep—not for flogging the flock. In Psalm 23, it says, "Thy rod and thy staff, they *comfort me.*" This was not an early S&M writing. Beating children is *NOT* the biblical message.

So anyway, I am not in favor of corporal punishment, and it *reeeally* pisses me off when people beat the crap out of their kids and try to blame it on the Bible. I believe the Bible teaches the exact opposite, in fact.

And in Ephesians 6:4, parents are further cautioned: "Fathers, do not provoke your children to anger, but bring them up in the discipline and instruction of the Lord." So there.

I suppose in cases of extreme danger—the kid darts out into the street—a quick swat on the hindquarters might be beneficial to the learning process. Kid will recall pain connected with running out into the street—if lucky enough to *not* be hit by car, will still get hit by freaked-out parent—so best to stay on the sidewalk.

But in most cases, I personally believe that the same lessons can be imprinted in the child's mind without the imprint of a hand on the child's body. Too often, I believe, hitting is the *first* option selected, and it's driven by anger and frustration and not a clear-headed desire to teach something to the child. Can you recall a time when your mom or dad whacked you and they *weren't* mad?

My friend Robin, Queen of Memphis and the Surrounding Area, said this friend of hers came into choir practice one night, marveling to herself about how her fairly bad four-year-old had skated on what looked like a pretty solid conviction for buttheadedness that day. This particular mama was a confirmed spanker, and she had him across her lap about to whale on him, and he turned his head up and said, "Mom, can you sing 'Happy Birthday' to me while you do it so it won't hurt so bad?" She laughed so hard she had to set him on the floor before she dropped him. Smart kid. *Genius,* maybe.

Although I believe we are commanded to teach our children with love and not force, I have found *no* such catechismal admonitions against scaring the crap out of them. Whenever

225

my own darling daughter, BoPeep, was a wee one and was acting buttheaded—which was, definitely and thankfully, a relatively rare occurrence—if The Look didn't work (more on this
in a moment), I would squat down right beside her and give her
The Look, up close, then I would whisper in her little bitty ear,
"*You* are embarrassing me and if you do not *stop it* this very second, then I am going to do something which will embarrass *you*
to such an extent, I'm not certain you will ever fully recover
from it." And I would resume my upright posture and carry on
with whatever activity her buttheadedness had interrupted—
undisturbed, I might add, by any further pint-sized unpleas-
antness.

I never had to follow through—and it's a good thing, too—
because I had *no plan* whatsoever for what my retaliatory hu-
miliating act would actually be. She never put it to the test. I
always assumed it was because I was such a major source of
embarrassment to her just being my regular self—no anger or
rancor attached—well, God *knows* what I might do if provoked.
Whatever. It worked—I care not why nor how.

Another good thing about whispering—it's real easy to make
it scary-sounding. Think Clint Eastwood—is your kid feeling
lucky today? Also, if your threats, veiled or otherwise, are normally couched in barely audible tones, when you do feel compelled to raise your voice (yell, holler, bellow, screech, scream,
etc.), it is a rare event and therefore garners much more attention.

Almost every mother can attest, with no small degree of irritation, that the *very* same instructions, demands, and/or warnings that they themselves have issued to their children endlessly and fruitlessly all day long are instantly heeded and obeyed with one single utterance by the father. Take whatever comfort you can from this: There's nothing magical about a proclamation from him, he's just an Unknown Quantity.

In most families, even today, the mother carries the primary weight of child rearing. She is the one the kids see and interact with the most on a daily basis—so they know their limits with her—they know just *exactly* how much Mom can be pushed before there is hell to pay. They know this (because Mom has taught it to them) and they do not shrink from using it.

Dad, on the other hand, they're not so sure about—so fine, they'll humor him, do what he says, he'll be gone soon enough—why risk it?

Driving home after a town excursion with her two daughters, Queen Jan stopped her car for an oncoming school bus to deposit some very slow-moving schoolkids on a corner. Jan glanced over at her baby daughter, and saw, to her horror, a giant black hairy spider creeping up the side of the car seat that held the so-far peacefully sleeping infant.

Silently blessing those snail's-paced students for affording her the time for this summary execution, Jan began slapping and whacking away at the beast. The noise of all this percussion on the frame of her car bed aroused the baby, who was at first startled awake by the noise and vibration of the whackage, but has now seen her mother's fierce facial expression up close and, believing herself to be under attack, sets up a deafening yowl, which, in turn, causes the older child buckled in the back-seat to commence screaming as well.

Jan's erratic swats at the spider somehow sent it sailing into the backseat, where it landed, of course, right next to the other child. As it began to head straight for her, Jan rapidly re-grouped and redirected her assault to the rear of the car. Both children were screaming like they were scared witless or on fire or both, and the bus driver, severely displeased at the scene be-fore her, leaned heavily and lengthily on her extremely loud bus horn—which did nothing to soothe either the bawling babies or Jan—who did finally manage to slay the beast with her bare hands.

Right hand scraping the carcass off the seat where it had come frightfully close to her frantic child, Jan's left hand was already pressing her window button to facilitate disposal of the remains. As Jan turned from the backseat with the carcass, her peripheral vision alerted her to the very close presence of a large, sweaty, and angry woman, engaged in the upward rolling of her own sleeves—as if in preparation for battle herownself.

Jan swiftly surveyed the scene and surmised in an instant that the entire population of the now-parked school bus—including the burly bus driveress—were convinced that they were witnessing an horrific public display of child abuse right before their very eyes in the middle of the street. Many of the children on the street and at the bus windows were crying as loud as her own kids, and Jan was about to get her ass kicked by one very pissed-off chauffeur.

Fortunately, before the ass-kicking could commence, Jan was able to avert this personal disaster by producing exonerating evidence — the dead body of ole Itsy Bitsy.

The Look

Every person who ever had a significant adult in their life can recall The Look. Maybe your mother had it, maybe it was your dad, your aunt, your grandmother — but somebody older than you had a particular facial expression that could immobilize you momentarily.

Desperate to rid herself, even temporarily, of the constant nagging presence of the little cocklebur that was me, Judy, always advanced for her age, had developed The Look before she even reached puberty. I'm certain this is some kind of world record, but I tried to Google it and found nothing.

At any rate, Judy would first fix me with a smoldering glare — withering, if you will — and then she would narrow her big blue eyes to mere snakelike slits, and I swear she could bend spoons and stuff with that Look. Judy's arsenal was not limited solely to The Look, however. If she didn't get the desired result — the sight of my swiftly fleeing backside going out the door to her room—then she would grab my arm and pull me close and, never releasing me from the grip of her eyes, she would hiss at me, "*You're* gonna wake up one of these mornings and look over there in your bed and *there you're gonna be—DEAD!*" It was pretty effective, at least for a brief spell, and she was careful not to overuse it and risk me becoming immune to its power, which I can assure you I never did—given that I'm nearly fifty-five and I can still feel her fingers on my arm, hear the venom in her whisper, and see the steely glint in her eyes.

(All that being said, I am happy to report that once Judy left home, I became more *tolerable* to her, and then somehow when I was in my twenties, I apparently underwent some kind of transformation and became *acceptable* in her sight. We have been absolute unwavering best friends ever since. She lives about two hundred miles away from me in New Orleans, but we have talked on the phone several times a day for the last thirty years. Even before long distance became affordable, our frequent conversations were a spiritual and budgetary necessity.)

Every parent needs to cultivate his or her own version of The Look, and this is something you absolutely *must have—before* you have children. If you are thinking now is the time for you to start a family, then there is simply no time to waste—you *must* get your Look perfected predelivery of the first child.

Practice in front of a mirror first and then try out your favorites with a close friend or partner. Have them help you select the scariest ones and try them out in public on selected strangers—targeting adults only for the test runs. (Hint: If you are, in fact, in the process of trying to conceive, it's probably best to try out your Look on persons other than the partner with whom you are attempting to launch this manufacturing venture—could be self-defeating otherwise.) Might I suggest the woman attempting to enter the express checkout line with more than fifteen items, the guy who whips into the parking space you've been waiting for, or all the people keeping their bus seats while the old lady and the pregnant woman have to stand, clinging to the straps, trying not to fall down—try your meanest looks on this ilk, and if you're successful in cowing them without a word, then you're ready to tackle children. (Not literally, you understand.)

I suppose it is not entirely too late for you if you already have some kids on hand and have failed somehow to cultivate your Look in advance. Actually, it's possible it will be an even more powerful weapon in your hands—or on your face, as it were—since you will have the added benefit of extreme *shock* value when, having been a mild-mannered and predictable pushover, you suddenly debut *The Look* for the little beesters.

Scared Straight

You never know from whence help might come to you as a parent. Just take it and be grateful for it when it does. My good friend Cherry was uneasy about the upcoming field trip her daughter Channon's class was taking—to a prison. Cherry had no idea what might be seen and heard by the teenagers in such a place, never having been inside one herownself.

And, in fact, Channon did come home from the tour visibly shaken and upset by the experience. Seeking some all-too-rare reassuring snuggle time with her mama (Cherry was at least grateful for that), Channon whispered, "Mama, I don't *ever* want to go to prison." (Another totally positive outcome here.) "Why not, darlin'?" Cherry asked. Channon closed her eyes and shuddered at the horrific memory of what she had witnessed that day, "*Oh, Mama*—they make you wear *long* blue jeans *all* the *time* and *they don't have air-conditioning*!" Fine, whatever it takes to keep 'em unincarcerated—ain't nothin' but a blessin'. And hey, excellent opportunity for some pithy hell analogies here as well.

Of course, for some children, the mere threat of being confined someplace really hot—in this life or the next—is insufficient as an attention grabber. Some of our children just *will* touch the hot stove, no matter what. It's why the makers of Xanax are justifiably billionaires.

Lynn thought she'd dodged a speeding bullet when she discovered a tiny bag of pot in her seventeen-year-old son's possession. Confronted with the evidence, Sonnyboy assumed the most common defense—the fallback position known as Deny, Deny, Deny. Okay, he used up the first two Denies when it was

obviously genuine marijuana and it was obviously in his *hand* —
he used his third one to declare that, okay, it really was weed
and he really was in possession of it — but *it wasn't really his* — he
was just "holding it for a friend."

Come on now, kid — you are supposed to be so much
smarter than all us old geezers — can't you come up with something a tad more original? Who, in the history of being caught
red-handed with contraband has *not* claimed to be merely holding it for a friend? It's not enough that you risk not only the ru-
ination of your own reputation but ours as well, your own
incarceration and ours, and financial ruin by way of legal fees
awaits the entire family tree, but you've got to *insult* us as well
with *this* pathetic excuse for a lie? And what a complete imbe-
cile that *friend* must be if he didn't think he could do a better job
himself of concealing the stash than you've done here — sitting
on the side of your bed with it in plain sight, *in your hand*, igmo.

So, round and round they went, and Sonnyboy was
grounded for all eternity and threatened with dismemberment
and assorted other atrocities for any future acts of stupidity,
and his parents came away from the event with sore backs from
all the congratulatory pats they swapped over their swift and
astute handling of what could have been a disastrous teenage
situation. All was well in their fiefdom once more — they so
foolishly thought.

The grounding eventually wore off. (Note to parents:
When you ground a kid, you're also grounding *yourself* — the

grounder—as the enforcer of said grounding must be on the premises to ensure absolute adherence to the groundation by the groundee.) Sonnyboy did not even allow his parents the span of anything like a decent interval—during which they could continue to congratulate themselves on their wisdom and efficacy as parents—before he pulled his next caper.

Lynn had a need for a phone book, and when searches of all logical locations for one proved futile, her last resort took her to the bedroom of her young criminal. There, indeed, she did find the wayward phone book—under a wad of dirty clothes—and on top of a big black plastic bag. One look inside sent her reeling back against the wall. She thought she'd stumbled onto the set of *Law & Order*—any second, she would hear the signature "dohn-dohn's" and Briscoe and Green would be coming to cuff her.

The bag held a one-pound *brick* of marijuana—she recognized it right off—it looked just like it does on TV—and it was on the short list of the last things she ever expected to find under the phone book in her own home. A quandary of the first order—closely related to any one of the circles of hell—was what she found herself in—herself and her big ole bag o' dope.

How to get rid of it—without getting caught with it? Flushing occurred to her—but she was afraid the big ole wads of weed would clog the pipes, and then there'd be the whole issue of a suitable explanation for the Roto-Rooter guy. She was afraid that burial might result in a spontaneous crop eruption in her backyard after the next good rain. She even thought about taking it to the *mall* and throwing it in a garbage can, but she was afraid she'd get caught with it on the way—and then *she'd* be forced to use the old "holding it for a friend" line, and she knew that if *she* hadn't bought that one, there was no chance of selling it to her arresting officer.

It was after eleven p.m. at Lynn's house at the end of the dead-end street as she went out to her backyard deck and fired up the gas grill. She put the brick in a shoebox full of newspaper, placed it on the grill rack, *set it on fire,* and closed the lid. Then she called Sonnyboy and invited him to run on home to join her, fireside.

Talk about your rock and your very hard place! Sonnyboy had no sanctuary. Home was not safe—his *mother* had found a solid felony's worth of weed in his room—she was not likely to be in her Nurturing Mom frame of mind. She had just set fire to what amounted to a couple of grand of *somebody else's* money. This time, he really *was* "holding it for a friend"—although he was also supposed to be *selling* it for a friend. Friend was gon' be wantin' his *cash* and would not be carin' overmuch about the fact that no merchandise had been moved—just liquidated, or incinerated, as it turned out. Sonnyboy had that pot on "consignment," and it was expected that he would deliver to Friend either the dollars or the doobie in a day or two. Friend was not going to be in an understanding frame of mind when he was told that "my mom burned it up on the barbecue grill," which, you have to admit, does smack of "the dog ate my homework," which also never works.

It wasn't like he could call the cops to report the theft. He had no choice but to drag his sorry little penny-ante, pissant drug-dealing ass *home* to *Mama* with the knowledge that he'd be lucky to still draw breath come morning—forget about standing by the fire and *inhaling*. If ever there was an "all for naught" situation—this was it.

Lynn doesn't even know how many minimum-wage hours Sonnyboy had to work—at a legitimate menial after-school job—to pay off that drug dealer, but it was enough to cure him. Bullet *finally* dodged—Sonnyboy is a productive citizen today. We can only hope he has children of his own while Lynn is still around to enjoy a little of his Karmic Comeuppance.

Aversion Therapy for the Awful Adolescent

When an older child is engaging in activities unsavory to the adults in his or her life, much thought must be given to the most effective response. When the motormouth of young Daniel was disrupting his fourth-grade teacher's attempts to teach, a note was sent home to his vigilant mom, Alycia, who, as it happened, had a plan for Daniel's *rehabilitation* already in mind. The family had recently moved to a new home, the front yard of which contained an enormous sweet gum tree. These trees produce soothing summer shade, spectacular fall foliage, and about 8 million little spiky "gumballs" per branch. The entire lawn was liberally littered with the pesky spheres. Firm but ever merciful, Alycia went out with a ball of twine and, after marking off a small section of the yard, summoned her errant son. He was instructed to pick up every single solitary gumball in that section and place it in the garbage bag she handed him along with a big bottle of Gatorade. Other than to use the restroom, he was not to stop or come inside until his section was absolutely 100 percent gumball free.

It took several miserably hot hours of either bending over or sitting on the very lumpy, spiky gumball-covered ground to pick them all up in just that one small section.

The next morning, as he walked out to catch the school bus, Alycia accompanied him and pointed to a newly cordoned off section of the yard. "That's in case you get to feelin' chatty in class *today*." Teacher sent home another message, this time saying Daniel had been *so* well behaved that day, she thought it was worthy of another note.

Year number sixteen in the life of dear Dominique's daughter was a memorable one for everyone in their small town. Daughter, knowing Mom to sleep deep and deadlike, decided it would be *the* easiest thing imaginable to purloin the Mom-mobile—a precious baby-blue BMW—for some serious about-town entertainment for herself and her best friend. And she was totally right—Dominique slept through the whole caper—

but what Daughter did *not* make a mental note of was the fact that Mom also got up while the chickens were still deep in dreamland.

And so it came to pass that as DomMom was coming down the stairs in the predawn dark to rustle up a cup of coffee for herself, she heard a sound she should not have been hearing emanating from the back door of the town house. It was the sound of that door opening.

Armed with a good-sized umbrella, Dominique crept to the foot of the stairs, eased across the living room to a spot just around the corner from the back door, assumed as menacing a posture as one can muster when one is armed with only rain gear, and shouted as fiercely as possible something along the lines of *"Freeze or I'll shoot!"*

From the ensuing racket, Dominique determined quite a few things without even turning the corner: There was more than one intruder; they were female; they were really surprised; they were heavily intoxicated. Half of the drunk duo was Dominique's daughter—the other half was her best friend.

As Mom rounded the corner, she saw something in her daughter's hand that froze her soul at the same time that it sparked her fury—car keys. *Not only* had they taken her beautiful baby-blue vintage BMW without permission—they had been drinking and, furthermore, they had been *driving while drinking* and apparently all night long.

Dom called the friend's mother and gave her the full report, told friend to wait on the front porch to be picked up by her own none-too-happy parents, and, to prevent any premature Mother-Daughter violence, sent her own daughter upstairs while she called her ex, the dad, to get over there and assist in the neck-wringing.

The parents of the little felon on the front porch arrive about the same time as Dad. Many long faces in this crowd. Nobody is having *any fun* in this neighborhood this morning. Drunk Daughter descends the stairs to face the united wrath of her parents. Dad decides that what is really needed here is a very long and boring lecture. After about an hour, Dominique decides that since *she* is about to fall asleep herownself, the likelihood that any of this endless droning is having any rehabilitative effect on a drunk teenager is nearly nil.

Daughter has been up all night long and is, in fact, still quite clearly as drunk as that ole Cooter Brown was always reputed to be. Dominique interrupts the dad's rant and tells the little lush to hop up and go fetch the scissors. Dad and daughter both look at her like she's grown a few more heads and eyes, but Dominique insists—get your drunk ass up and go get the scissors. Daughter stumbles into the kitchen and returns, scissors in hand, bewildered look on face. Mom orders her outside to cut the grass. With the scissors. That time-honored teenage look of Unmitigated Surliness makes a momentary appearance on the face of the Daughter—but it is immediately overpowered and soundly trounced by *The Look* on Dominique's face, which assures all that death is imminent for someone and it doesn't much matter whose it is.

And so, Dominique got her lawn truly manicured. Granted, it was a town house, so there was not exactly a meadow to mow — but when the only tool for the job is a set of kitchen shears, it can drag on. Did we mention that by this time it was eightish in the a.m.? Daughter had been out all night long, she was still drunk, and she'd just been sent out on this bright, sunshiny, already-hot-as-the-hammered-down-hinges August morning — in Alabama — to cut the grass with the scissors.

It took her until around noon to finish. Dominique did take her lots of water to make sure that, as tempting as it had been earlier, she didn't *actually* kill the child. When the youthful bacchanalian dragged her bedraggled body into the house — nothing but bed on her mind — she was met by Mom, holding out a toothbrush — with which she was instructed to scrub the floors in the kitchen and bathrooms, and *then* she could go to bed to sleep it off.

This is a most excellent example of Aversion Therapy. For most of us in the South, the smell of freshly cut grass is sweet perfume and the scent of a newly washed floor is a soul-soothing reminder of the comforts of home — intoxicating odors, if you will. But for at least one little girl in Alabama, a whiff of either one will, for all her life, remind her of scissors and toothbrushes — and her doomed dance with Demon Rum.

Manners Matter

In the South, you will sometimes hear it said of a person, "Yew cain't take he-um *inny*-whur." Directly translated into English: "You cannot take him anywhere." It means that the person in question is best left at home, and if he's not, he can be counted upon to embarrass the person foolish enough to ignore this warning.

Also frequently heard in the South: "How yew gon' act whin yew git sum-whur?" This is most often uttered through clenched adult teeth and directed at a young'un who is experiencing a preemptive "butthead interruptus" procedure involving a yanked arm and/or swatted behind—and is considered to be a rhetorical question only and certainly not one for which the alleged butthead should attempt to formulate and verbalize an answer at that particular time. When this question is asked, the adult has already mentally answered it for him/herself prior to voicing it—and the answer is, of course, "*This* is how you act when I take you out," which brings up the whole "cain't take he-um any-whur" thing once more.

Personally, I believe that nobody—of any age—should be taken anywhere until they know how to act upon arrival and for the duration. And furthermore, at the very moment that it becomes painfully apparent to anybody within fifty miles with a working eyeball or eardrum that someone does *not*, in fact, know how to behave in the current environment, that individual should be *removed* immediately and with all haste.

Yes, children learn from experience. When they experience a swift and sure "party's over" at the first display of unacceptable behavior in a public place, they will then learn to resist the urge to act buttheaded. They do *not* learn this by being allowed to remain in the middle of the store, party, restaurant, park— wherever—while pitching a hissy fit and having their parents try to "reason" with them. And, by the way, it may well "take a village" to raise a child, but the "village" never gets to vote, and if we *did*, it would be unanimous—*TAKE THAT AWFUL KID OUTTA HERE...NOW!*

Nobody else signed on to help you bring up your child. We understand that you are focused on trying to teach an important "life lesson"—we don't care—all we want is peace and quiet. It is not our problem that little Angel gets bored sitting at the dinner table like a human. Get a babysitter or stay at home and teach little Angel some manners before you inflict her on the public. Go eat pizza at Chuck E. Cheese—they encourage simian-like behavior there.

My nephew Trevor and his bride, RuthAnna, are going to take their three children, Riley, Conner, and Mason—all under age six—on a "fancy" vacation at a very famous resort this summer. The children understand that there exist Major Parental Expectations Regarding Their Behavior during this time, and so the family has been having "practice runs." Starting with local casual dining establishments in their hometown of New Orleans with successful outings leading to successively upscale eateries, the troupe recently went to the fabulous Marriott's Grand Hotel in Point Clear, Alabama—only a short drive from New Orleans—for a full weekend of public performances of perfect comportment. This was to be the last drill and it was felt that success here would mean it was safe to spend Big Money on the Real Deal. To fork over exorbitant sums of U.S. Dollars just to sit in a hotel room (albeit a five-star, very expensive one) with an ill-behaved brood was not an appealing thought. (It must be said that The Grand—as it's universally known—is itself a five-star resort and spa, so it ain't like they were practicing at the Red Roof Inn—but since it's within easy driving distance they knew they wouldn't also be wasting expensive airfare if things didn't go well. If it all went to crap, they'd just throw the kids back in the car and haul 'em home for more practice. Most happily, this did not prove to be necessary.)

Saturday night dinner in the Grand Dining Room of the hotel is worth the drive—no matter what your starting point. It's comfortably elegant and the views are spectacular. Our little family arrives for this, the Grand Finale—how WILL these young'uns act, now that they *are* somewhere. Everyone is seated and several courses are served without a single hitch, hoot, or holler. The menu items are described for the kids and *actual* meals are selected and consumed (no plain hamburgers or cheese pizzas) by the children. The adults order and enjoy their own dinners—and even a bottle of wine. No children *anywhere* have ever been better behaved in the history of the *en*-tire world. It was a miracle of Early Childhood Education is all it was. The kids talked pleasantly to one another and were polite to the adults at their own table, the staff, and those in the immediate area.

The same could not be said of everyone in the room.

There was, across the way, a table of young men—early twenties, college-frat-boys-on-spring-break types—who had been imbibing heavily and growing louder with every round of drinks, but so far everybody had been able to pretty much ignore them, and our little ones were happily nattering away, paying no attention whatsoever to the grown-up buttheads at that table. All of a sudden, something *very exciting* evidently happened at the butthead table—like maybe more drinks arrived—because there was a sudden deafening group shout that reverberated across the hall.

The little *well-behaved children* were so shocked by the sound that they froze, mid-sentence, eyes big and round, and they gasped. As if on cue, they whipped their little heads around, and turned their little bodies in their chairs and their startled gazes to the butthead table across the way. With a disapproving and disgusted air, they slowly turned away from the scene of the etiquette disaster and continued Behaving Well.

Everyone in the dining room witnessed it — the shock and dismay of the *little children* at the rude behavior of the adults — and there was much laughter at the expense of the buttheads and many congratulations to Trev and RuthAnna *and* the kids on being the Nicest Table in the room. After a few minutes, the whole table of buttheads, now properly chagrined, made their way over to Trev's table — to *apologize* to the *children* for their be- havior — which did provide such a glowing example of how *not* to act whin yew git sum-whur.

A Prime Example of What "Assuming" Will Do for You

You've all heard the old saw that goes "When you *assume* something — you make an *ass* out of *U* and *ME*." And there are plenty of good reasons why that BECAME an "old saw." Here's one example: Queen Molly was working with her baby girl, Molly II or MollyTwo, as she's called, on the important life lesson of showing one's appreciation for kindness and consideration extended to one. A sincere "Thank you" was the desired response Molly was seeking and the one she foolishly *assumed* she would get from MollyTwo when the drive-thru bank lady sent a lollipop through the tube with Molly's money and receipt. "What do you say to the nice lady?" Molly prompted. MollyTwo climbed over and leaned across Molly's torso to yell into the microphone, *"I want two!"* One of them at least certainly learned *that* lesson the first time—thereafter, Molly was more explicit in her instructions: "Tell the nice lady, *'Thank you.'*"

Suffer the Little Children to Come unto the Nursery

Yes, Jesus said it, bring on the babies and all that—but he *was* out in a *field* somewhere when he said it. I bet if He was trying to sit in a roomful of people and listen to a preacher try to talk over a screaming baby, He'd be looking around for the Cry Room HisOwnSelf. I really do not think that He was issuing a wholesale endorsement of wagging little kids anywhere and everywhere all the time. If your baby sleeps through the whole thing, great—otherwise, please slip out quietly and quickly.

And *please,* do not bring toddlers or anybody else who is physically and mentally incapable of sitting for one hour (sometimes a bit more) *without talking.* If your child is working the puzzles from Sunday school—and has to ask you every question—and you are *answering* every question—then *neither of you* is listening to the sermon—so *why are you in there,* bugging the crap out of everybody around you? If you and your child want to have a conversation—*go somewhere else*—and you won't even have to whisper!

I need to *hear* what that apple-headed preacher is trying to tell me or I wouldn't be there. I am *not* thinking "Christian" thoughts at *all* when you and your child are talking and rustling papers and kicking the back of my *pew* the whole time.

Send the little ones to Sunday school and from thence to the nursery if you are going to go to Big Church. A two-three-four-five-year-old cannot understand what is being said, has no interest in what is being said, and it is *cruel* to them *and* to everybody in a four-row radius to try to force them to do what is *physically impossible* for them to do at that age—sit still and be quiet for sixty-some-odd minutes in a row.

Put adult-centered movies on your Do Not Do List as well. Not only do they ruin the experience for every adult in the theater, there is a fairly high risk of them absorbing material that is unsuitable for their age group. (You would think that we would have learned *something* from our collective "Prince Charming" experiences, wouldn't you? How many of you are *still* waiting for him? Let's be a little more careful what we plant in our children's brains.)

Now, *As Good As It Gets* with Jack Nicholson and Helen

Hunt is one of my all-time favorite movies. I think it was perfectly written, perfectly cast, and perfectly performed. When it was released, my daughter was well under the recommended age for viewing audiences and I wouldn't let her watch it, despite her pleadings. I explained to her that she wouldn't "get" most of it—and that I didn't want it ruined for her—she could watch it when she was old enough to appreciate the story.

A little girl, Sherrie, the daughter of one of Judy's New Orleans friends, *was* allowed to watch it and she was totally intrigued by the obsessive-compulsive behaviors of Nicholson's character—so much so, Judy told me, that the child began to *imitate them.* And her parents played along—hovering anxiously, hauling her to therapists and indulging her in her "rituals." One of our closest lifelong friends had been racked with OCD her entire adult life—we had observed it plenty close up. Judy and I strongly suspected that this child was performing.

When little Sherrie announced that she "could not" get out of Judy's car until she put the window up and down five times and touched every metal surface with her left hand, Judy employed our own mama's favorite therapy model—Judy said to her, "*Oh, baloney*—get out of the car." And whaddya know? She got out of the car and was not the least bit "tormented" by the interruption of her "compulsive ritual." Turned out, she really only had "episodes" at *home*—where there was a receptive audience.

(As I said, I am well aware that OCD is a genuine crippling affliction for many, and I am not suggesting for an instant that they "snap out of it," since I know that they would if they could but they can't. My point is children are sponges and they do soak up everything around them—from us, from movies, from TV—and they sometimes "try it on." What I believe they need from us—at least on the front end—is guidance and assurance that they are *not* crazy. Everybody has thoughts that would be undesirable, unacceptable, and/or unlawful if carried into action. Kids need to know that everybody *does* have those thoughts—and that's normal. It's what we *do* with those thoughts that matters. If your child needs professional help, by all means, get it sooner rather than later—but at least give common sense a *try* before rushing off in a panic to hand your child off for the therapy du jour.)

Mama didn't have a therapist, didn't know anybody who had one, and didn't watch TV shows that glamorized goofy behavior in grown-up people. I take that back, she did watch *As the World Turns* for about ten years until it got too "far-fetched" for her taste. That probably would have been about the time adultery, drug addiction, and the existence of a previously unknown evil twin became regular plot lines in the soaps.

"Oh, baloney" was what my mother had to say about anything she felt smacked of self-indulgent, self-pitying, sitting-down-in-the-middle-of-the-road-waiting-for-somebody-to-come-along-and-rescue-me behavior. She expected adults—especially parents—to act in adultlike fashion: You get up, you do your work for the day, you handle whatever comes your way, you

eat, you go to bed—you repeat daily for however many years you are allotted on this earth. Childless persons were given slightly more leeway since their behavior was seen to have no adverse effects on minor children—but once you had kids, you were expected to buck the hell up and *deal* with life. And that's pretty much what she and most of her contemporaries did.

Fortunately for us—their children—Paris Hilton, Britney Spears, and the like were not yet role models.

There was the occasional "nervous breakdown" in the ranks. I have yet to learn what this entailed—never heard a set of symptoms described, let alone a course of treatment. It was simply announced (in hushed tones, over the neighborhood telephone lines) that "Lydia had a nervous breakdown." One of us kids would overhear it and spread the news to the rest of the junior citizens, and it was understood from that moment on that Lydia's house was off-limits. The children of Lydia could still come to *our* houses to play—although they were "watched"—but none of us was allowed to go there—pretty much ever again. It was as if Lydia had some communicable and highly unattractive disease—she was up the street in Lydia's Leper Colony from thenceforth and forevermore.

Perhaps if Mama and Lydia had been closer friends, Lydia could have confided her woes and been given and perhaps even healed by the sage, universal salve Mama applied to all such scenarios: *"Oh, baloney."*

I did receive similar counseling once from the late, great

Maggie Lay, an actual trained and certified therapist, when I wailed to her that I simply "could not stand" whatever was going on in my life that brought me to her door. She looked at me calmly and advised me that I *was*, in fact, standing it. Pulled me up short, mid-snuffle, I admit. She went on to say that just because I was *choosing* to "stand it" upside down with my hair on fire, none of my dramatics was having the slightest impact on the situation at hand—suggesting that I might want to just maybe consider the possibility of identifying it and then *taking* some positive action about it myownself.

I did not get any "poor you" messages from Maggie. She would not agree with me that the situation was, indeed, hopeless. She would not affirm for me that this particular situation had probably, in her opinion, never happened to another person in the history of humans on the earth and certainly not in *her* practice. Rather, she seemed to be almost bored with my little problem—as if it were the thousandth time that *week* she'd heard of something similar—and there was no counting it over the span of her esteemed career. How she must have longed for a real tragedy or two—some genuine incapacity in her clients.

She discussed with me the two or three blatantly *obvious* solution tracks I could choose from—gently badgered me until I chose one—and then booted me out to *live* my life. Said she was not interested in "taking people to raise." In Maggie's opinion, if you had a problem for which you—a bona fide adult—could not arrive at a reasonable course of action in three months or less—even with the aid of a licensed therapist—you probably needed in-patient treatment. She said, "Life just *isn't* as hard as we would like to paint it—otherwise we would be a whole lot *smarter.*"

Very often, we are not actually *looking* for a *solution*—we just want an *excuse* to continue our current insanity. A good therapist's response to "It hurts when I do this" is "Don't do that." And if you are *truly* incapable of stopping yourself, then you probably need to be hospitalized. Sooner or later, one way or another, it all comes down to the moment when we actually *choose to stop doing that.* Maggie's theory was that we ought to stop sooner rather than later and we ought to stop it without medicinal assistance.

Sounds suspiciously like *"Oh, baloney"* to me.

Riding in the SUV to Hell

Parenting magazines are just full up with articles written by actual paid columnists as well as letters sent from moms (Alpha, no question)—all containing "helpful" hints for entertaining our children while transporting them from point A to point B in a moving vehicle, which we ourselves are *driving.* Most of these "hints" involve car games consisting of handmade paper and intricate artwork—craft projects—which, by the way, are *so much fun* to make *with* your children. So it's a total twofer—

win/win—whoo-hoo situation—*before* you go anywhere in the car, you can spend several hours of high-quality time with your children constructing the games for them to play *in* the car while you're driving.

I don't have any instructions for these to offer you here and now—but you can find *tons* of them online at www.bite-me.com, I'm sure. (Okay, I made up that Web site—don't actually go there looking for parenting tips.)

Who cannot recall those *endless* family car trips from their childhood? I can still vividly remember leaning up from the backseat (seat belts had not even been *invented* then), head thrown back, whining—I can still feel the pressure in my neck and throat caused by the position and the tone—"How *minnie-more miles* is it?" "*Whi-i-in* are we gonna *git* there?" If I asked it once, I asked it a thousand times—and the answer never mattered. Unless we were driving up to the destination at that precise moment, it was not the answer I wanted and thus no relief was afforded to my poor, beleaguered parents.

Queen Hannah had similar childhood memories of pestering her parents, asking over and over and over, "Are we there yet? Are we there yet? Aren't we there *yet*?" Until finally one day, her mom snapped. Hannah asked, "Are we there yet?" just one too many times and Mama swerved to the side of the road, slammed on the brakes, and said, "*Yes*—get out!" Hannah recollects that was the very last time she ever asked her mama that question.

Meet Tom Sawyer's Little Sister, Christy

Our Christy is a devout Beta—freely admits that her boys (ten and seven) have watched *plenty* of TV during those times when she just had to have a quiet personal moment or several. However, she has made a very fine silk purse out of the ear of that particular sow by harnessing the gadget-lust engendered in her boys' hearts by the advertising and telemarketing pundits of America and turning it loose in her dirty kitchen.

It came about in complete innocence, actually, when she had run by Wal-Mart on her way to work one morning and in her hunt for big giant Ziploc bags she wandered into the cleaning aisle and There It Was—calling her name. She'd seen the ads herownself and was admittedly quite lured. Now that she was standing here in front of it—and it was only thirty-eight dollars—how could she be expected to resist it? In true Mom-style, elevating the needs of others above her own, Christy thought to herself, "I bet the boys would *love* this!" And it went home with her that very day.

I'm talking about the Swiffer SweeperVac, ladies and gentleman. It's like a Dustbuster/mop combo, and to a gadget junkie it's heroin. Want it bad. Gotta have it.

When she arrived at the homeplace with it, the conversation went a little something like this:

BOYS: OOOOOOOH! COOOOOL!

What is it? Is this one of those *Swiffer* things on TV?
Can we use it?

CHRISTY: No. It's mine. Besides, it has to charge twenty-four
hours.

Somehow, even with the excitement of their very own *Swiffer*
silently sucking up and storing power, girding its loins for the
fray, everyone manages to sleep that night.

Next morning —

BOYS: Can we use the Swiffer?

CHRISTY: No. I told you it was *mine*, and besides, it hasn't
been twenty-four hours yet. Y'all can use it *if* I say you
can and only after we finish cleaning up after supper.
Besides, you don't use it *every time*, those Swiffer pads
are expensive.

(She has staked out her territory plus she has introduced the
idea that they will have to *earn* their Swiffer privileges by performing Quests That She Demands, and she has put them on
notice that they will not *ever* get to use it as much as they want
to — so now they are *panicking* to use it as much as possible —
may even be willing to sneak around and clean behind her back
and then lie about it later.)

Later that day —

BOYS: Can we use it *now*?

> CHRISTY: No. We're eating out tonight. Remember, we *only* use it after we finish cleaning up from supper.

Two days later—the boys drag the Swiffer in after supper.

> BOYS: Can we use it now, *pleeeeze*?
>
> CHRISTY: No. We have to do First Things First. So . . . first, we put the leftovers away. Then we clean the table. Then we do the dishes. Cleaning the floor is the very last thing we do—*that's* when we use the Swiffer. Bring the leftovers from the table and put them on the counter. I'll put them away while y'all clean the table.

The Boys scramble for Mr. Clean and paper towels, arguing over who will spray and who will wipe, complete the job, then breathlessly demand to know what's next.

> CHRISTY: Dishes must be washed, dried, and put away.

If Mr. Clean, the Scrubbing Bubbles, and the Pine-Sol lady had worked in concert, those dishes could not have been dispatched any faster. Two eager little boy faces, beaming with pride in their jobs well and quickly done, turn to Christy for that Royal Dispensation they have been working toward and anticipating with such fervent desire: Permission to Use the Swiffer, Granted. The keys to Disneyland could hardly have been met with more enthusiasm—which, of course, immediately disintegrated into that age-old argument: Who gets to go first? Back and forth they went, with each lobbying staunch arguments for his own qualifications for First-Use Rights on the Swiffer. Christy ultimately had to intervene and threaten them with Prompt and Permanent Withdrawal of the Permission if it was going to cause such disharmony in her kitchen—she reminded them that the Swiffer belonged to *her.*

This nearly spawned an argument with each *insisting* that the *other* one go first. A coin was finally tossed and the Swiffering began in earnest. Christy did help fan the fires of their enthusiasm by suggesting various "tests" for the Swiffer: How far would it reach under the table? How close did you have to be to a bit of detritus for it to be sucked up? What was the turning radius? Between these and assorted evaluations of this new high-tech piece of equipment that was the sole property of Mom but she was so cool to let them actually play with, Christy's kitchen floor shone as bright as the smiles on her children's faces.

She slept the sleep of a Woman with a Perfectly Clean Kitchen—and also that of a Mom Satisfied That She Was, in Fact, Still Devious, Cunning, and Sufficiently Underhanded to Totally Get Over On a Couple of Little Boys. We salute her.

It's Just a Short Drive
to the Poorhouse

W here exactly *is* the "Poorhouse"? *Is* there such a place? Was there ever? During the entire time I lived with my parents, I reckon I heard the Poorhouse mentioned at least as many times as Heaven—probably more. We were headed there—to the Poorhouse, that is—on a greased downhill slope and I was driving the bus. This was, however, long before I ever even thought about learning to *drive*. (I was and always have been a very late bloomer—things other people did at age fifteen, I waited until I was twenty-two. Eventually I get around to stuff but never been in much of a hurry.)

If we weren't collectively going to the Poorhouse, then my mother was going solo to Whitfield, that being the name of the Mississippi facility for the mentally ill—or insane asylum, as we called it back then. Nobody knew from "mentally ill" when

I was growing up, you were just crazy. In any event, as a youngster, my "driving" time was equally divided between making sure that my family arrived as quickly as possible at the Poorhouse and qualifying my mother for a padded room at Whitfield.

Once I did learn to actually operate a motorized vehicle, my mother's estimated arrival times for both locations seemed to advance significantly. It is only *now*, as the mother of a teenager myownself, that I can even begin to comprehend what my mother meant by muttering about "the tortures of the damned."

You just think you worry about your children when they are little and you have an equal or perhaps greater misconception regarding the level of torment that you endure at their hands. Terrible twos? The mother of a teenager will laugh in your very face—she would/could take on ten or twelve two-year-olds concurrently for the rest of her LIFE and it wouldn't be a very tiny pimple on the very ample ass of Motherhood.

It is true—that ole saying you've heard—that the decision to have a child is the decision to have your beating heart just *out there*, walking around free in the world. Free and exposed to every danger ever thought of by a mother and more. But when they learn to *drive*—then you have your beating heart *out there*, but it's now *riding* on top of a four-thousand-pound *bomb*—if you are lucky, it's wearing a seat belt.

Somewhere around eleven to thirteen, the eyeballs of children become extremely loose in their sockets, so that just about any disturbance in the air around them—say, a *word* issuing forth from, say, *your mouth*—will cause immediate and severe rolling. Time and/or consequences will eventually cause the sockets to tighten up again so that their eyes remain facing forward, but I swear, for about five years there, my daughter looked like she was from the Village of the Damned—I saw nothing but the backs of her eyeballs, she kept 'em rolled up so far.

By the time they reach the end of their teen years, they will (sadly) know a good many people their own age who have suffered the horrendous consequences we have been warning them about since birth—and we as parents will have begun to emerge from the cocoon of Utter Stupidness they have perceived us to be swathed in for the last several years.

You've also heard it said that if giving birth was assigned to *men*, there would have been *one* baby born, and after that the word would have gotten around and the whole human race woulda died off right then. Well, God has also very cleverly withheld the whole *teenage* experience from parents until we've had all those years of bliss with our perfectly sweet, adorable *babies*—because if anybody *really knew* what they were in for— again, extinction would be just around the corner.

And my theory is that all of those sweet baby memories are like money in the bank and we survive on the interest those memories have built up over the early years—because we know and believe that our precious children are *in there some-where,* and that if we can just hold on and not murder them and/or ourselves, then sooner or later that precious person will reemerge and grace the world.

Remember this — it might save your child's life and your own. By that I mean, if you can just remember this one thing, it *might* prevent tomorrow's top local news from detailing a murder-suicide — at your house. Here's the deal: You know how when kids do something *reeeeally stupid* — I mean, something just so unbelievably dumb, so completely boneheaded, so totally mo-ronic — that also ends up costing a boatload of money for home and auto repairs, medical bills, and lawyers for bailing them out of it — *that* kind of stupid — and you ask them, for the love of God, *why* did they do this, and they look you dead square in the face and say, "I don't know." You know that scenario? You just want to — and perhaps do — *scream* at them, *"What do you mean, You DON'T KNOW?!"* And all they can say, yet again, is, "I don't know." Does this ring any familiar bells in your memory?

Well, it's the truth. *They Don't Know.* They have absolutely *no idea why* they did that stupid thing — and there is scientific *proof* that they don't know. The brain of an adolescent is *not* fully formed, and the part that isn't "done yet" is the part where we make the *impulse controls.*

The really bad news (for you) is that, most times, their brains aren't "done" until they're in their *twenties.* OMIGOD — how will you survive? Ahhh . . . I don't know.

But do keep this brain-development fact in mind—and share it with them as well. Who knows, maybe just having that fact planted in their brains will allow for the hopeful possibility that it could *pop up* when they're presented with the next stupid impulse—and maybe, just maybe, give them a moment's pause *before* committing the stupid act. It couldn't hurt.

(I personally believe that this scientific information shines an awful light on our Juvenile Justice System and that it must be addressed. I believe we are quite possibly creating a whole class of lifetime career criminals—out of children that our current laws are incarcerating as adults. It's certainly worth exploring, no?)

But enough of that—back to our story, Okay, so you've got this eye-rolling adolescent who wants the car keys and part of you just wants some *relief* so bad, you're tempted to just throw the keys at 'em and run back into the house. It was the opposite at our house because, as I said, I didn't drive until I was twenty-two. I hung around all the time, dispensing misery my every waking hour. I remember my seventeenth year like it was yesterday, and I still so clearly see my little pissant, eye-rolling self standing on the front porch, rotten attitude coming off me like dead-skunk funk, and my poor frazzled, menopausal mother, tearing out the door, leaving, saying she was going to "drive the car off a bridge," and me just standing there, all cool and aloof, going, "Bye!"

With the state of, shall we say, disharmony that usually exists between parents and their adolescent offspring, I would highly recommend that you hire a professional driving instructor when learner's permit time arrives at your house. It's just really not a good idea to take all of that conflict out for a ride in the family car—on the public roads.

I did make some initial forays into driving as a teenager, but my daddy—who did possess most of the patience allotted for this hemisphere—unfortunately traveled all the time and so there was no time for consistent driving practice with him. Mother, having suffered the soul-flaying brunt of Life with the Teenage Me, was hardly in the proper frame of mind to ride shotgun with me behind the wheel.

On one of our rare driving excursions when I was about fifteen, I recall being way more focused on relating to Daddy some endless teenage drama tale than I was on the road, and before I knew it, a "stopping" occasion came up on the road and I was going a little faster than I had been aware of and I probably came down a bit hard on the brake pedal and Daddy nearly went through the windshield.

That didn't bother him—he considered it part of the learning process, which it was, I suppose. What singed even his unassailable patience was my eye-rolling attitude of dismissal when he tried to discuss what had just happened and how it needed to be different in the future—proper speed, correct braking technique, and, above all, paying more attention to *driving* than anything else, like yakking. "I wasn't even going that *fast*," I whined. That, as they say, tore it for him as he tried, in vain, to explain how the weight of the car and the speed of the car made even the slightest impact a really Big Deal. This was met with mega eye-rolls and that *breathing* thing teenagers do—you know, the big, disgusted exhale thing.

So, Daddy said when we got home, here's the plan. Let's have a little $E = mc^2$ kinda lesson here. He asked me how fast I thought I could run in an absolute dead heat. I said I had no earthly idea. He said, oh, come on, make a guess, five miles per hour, even? You were going thirty when you hit the brakes— can you run that fast? Ahh, no. Well, how fast, then—what's the absolute fastest you can run? I still had no thoughts on the matter and my eyes were rolling so much it was making me drunk. No matter, he said, you see that wall of the house there? Duh, yeah—it's right there. Okay, then you go out to the street and you run, just as fast as you possibly can, straight into that wall, and let's see how you do.

Of course, I didn't actually *do* it—but the point of that lesson has stuck with me for more than forty years and I hardly ever run into stuff—on foot or in my car.

Housework Kills Plenty of People All the Time

Why, just the other day, my dear friend Alycia answered the phone sounding like she'd been out on a major toot all weekend long—very droopy and not at all her usual perky self. Naturally I inquired as to the specific cause and reason for her very audible slump. It seems that Alycia was partaking of some pretty significant pain-relief medications warranted by the fact that, over the previous weekend, she had not, after all, been out on a major toot—not even a minor one, not even out, as it turns out. She was, in a word, tootless.

After working all week outside the home, nothing would do for our Alycia but to then spend all weekend inside the home, neatening and straightening and scouring all the assorted crannies and nooks (or is it nannies and crooks?). The upshot of all that superfluous housecleaning is that she some-how pulled a muscle in her chest wall and now she's in so much pain she can hardly breathe and, like most people, Aly-cia breathes a lot—really all day, every day—and now it hurts real bad to do that.

See? I told her, do you *see now*? Even if she had not been drugged, she would not have seen—Alycia is a Cleaner—Aly-cia is an Alpha Cleaner. If she is Alpha, I am not even Beta— I would have to be that very last one—the Omega—that is how very far apart we are on the Compulsive Cleaning Scale. I am not *ever* compelled to clean—not by any inward yearning or drive anyway. Occasionally, I am compelled to create a pathway through the crap so I can get to the refrigerator or bathroom, but other than that, naw—no compulsion over here.

What I wanted Alycia to *see* was that *my* chest wall was not on fire—I was not requiring opiates in order to breathe—and this Should Be a Lesson Unto Her. Do Not Go Raking Out Closets When You've Already Put in a 40+-Hour Workweek— Sit Down and Rest Like a Normal Human or You Will Hurt Yourself. I should have a plaque made of that for her.

Talking to the wall, though—Alycia *will* clean and I *won't*— it's how we're made and we've spent our entire lives each *being* this way. We're not likely to change patterns for the balance of the time we have left to us.

For those of you starting out, though—there's still time and possibly hope for you. Your time can be better spent *being with* your families than cleaning up after them constantly. Try to meet the minimum hygiene standards—and by the way, get that family to *help* with that maintenance—and then go play with 'em and have a nice nap. Much better use of your time—trust me on this.

A friend of mine went to see, at my recommendation, Dr. Buddy Wagner at Mississippi College for a little help wrangling the snakes she had been harboring inside her head. Dr. Wagner is the best snake wrangler in the world, as far as I can tell. Friend-girl was ready to murder her family as soon as she could find a way to do it that would not sully her new white carpet—which had become the center of her universe. Everything in that household now revolved around that freaking white carpet—every potential action had to be considered in light of the effect it could possibly have on the white carpet. Her *family* was failing utterly to appreciate the many fine qualities and even the sublime beauty and perfection of the white carpet. They just thought it felt good to walk on—which was one of the main things she could not *bear* for them to do.

She liked to get in there and vacuum that carpet carefully so that all of the little tracks left by the vacuum lined up perfectly and the white carpet looked like a pristine field of virgin snow, covering the floors of the rooms and halls in her home. She liked to just sit and look at how perfect it was.

And then, the front door would open and shut, open and

shut, open and shut—indicating the home arrival of the assorted members of her family—and they would each in turn *walk* around, messing up the "snow," and she would be forced to redo it every morning to restore its flawless beauty.

This carpet obsession was irritating the crap out of her family, and their failure to comprehend the Zen of the white carpet was elevating her crabbiness to dangerous levels. Before there was blood on the carpet, I suggested she go have a little talk with Dr. Buddy.

She went, eagerly in fact, believing that the good doctor would help her figure out how to convince her family to embrace the preservation of the white carpet as their universal Reason for Being. The brilliant doctor conversed with her for a time until he felt he had a firm grasp on the issue at hand and then he asked her to do a little guided visualization.

She settled back in her chair and listened to his soft voice instructing her to close her eyes and mentally *see* her carpet in the way that made her the happiest. I'm sure the tension in her face and body fell away as she visualized that perfect field of snow in her living room. She was told to observe every nuance of its impeccable purity. This went on for a time and she was digging it, for sure.

Then he told her to realize *why* her carpet was so perfect. It was perfect because there *was nobody* to walk on it, to spill food on it, to *ruin it*—because she was absolutely and utterly *alone* with her white carpet. She would be able to keep it in its original flawless state forever—because she was the only one who would ever come in contact with it.

From behind her closed eyes, tears began to eke out, and she saw, finally, what Dr. Wagner wanted her to see—the glory of the footprints on her white carpet, made as they were by the precious feet of her most loved ones. There's always a different way of looking at things.

One of my very favorite Queens in all the World is Deborah McCoy-Freeman. In 2001, she persuaded a girlfriend to come with her to the Million Queen March at Mal's St. Paddy's Parade. The friend was all for it—until she realized that the event was in Jackson, Mississippi—which meant a twenty-two-hour drive from their home in Grand Forks, North Dakota—but they did it and I love 'em for it. I still remember looking out at that crowd and seeing their sign, NORTH DAKOTA LOVES THE SWEET POTATO QUEENS! Quite thrilling for a first-time author in the Deep South to know her work had been so well received so far from home.

Anyway, on Halloween, when Deborah's youngest, Krisanne, was four, it had been the subject of a Mom Decree that, while her big sis would wear some fancy finery brought home from her first-grade classroom—tutu, tiara, fairy wand, etc.— Krisanne was the Designated Clown Suit Wearer. Deborah had made the clown suit for her first child seven years earlier and it had been passed down through the ranks of subsequent children. This would be the last Halloween that Krisanne would fit into the clown costume and Deborah was determined to get that one last wearing out of the thing. Too bad for Krisanne—she should have grown faster, I suppose.

Krisanne's dad's only job was to somehow wrestle that clown suit on the kid before trick-or-treat time. Deborah was busy putting makeup on everybody else when she heard a minor commotion coming from down the hall, followed by Dad's exasperated final shot, *"Well, just go show your mother, then!"* Deborah knew from that one sentence that there had been a battle and a war between the four-year-old and her father and that he had not won either one of them. She tried to psych herself up for what she imagined was schlumping down the hall.

Opening the bathroom door, Deborah saw the little sad-sack face of baby Krisanne—she was wearing a twisted tutu, a crooked tiara, and fiercely clutched a stick wrapped in foil—she'd made herself a wand. Deborah asked the obvious question, "And what are you supposed to be?" Nearly in tears, Krisanne looked up and said, "A Fairly Good Mother."

"Oh, heck, baby, *so am I*—get in here and let's put some makeup on that face!"

Always another way of looking at life and figuring out what's *really* important. I can tell you this with absolute certainty: Nobody goes to the nursing home wishing they'd served on a few more committees or kept a cleaner house.

More Play, Less Fray

Play will help save from fraying that last intact nerve you still have to your name. Then you can look forward to time with your kids as "time for fun"—as opposed to "entering the fray."

Everybody breathing needs to play—almost as much as they need to breathe. University studies (I've got the article somewhere, but it's buried in my office, so just trust me) have shown that *play* is *as* important to our (humans) health and well-being as *food, clothing,* and *shelter.* All humans—all ages—not just kids.

Y'all know I preach the Power of Play constantly as one of the Basic Tenets of Sweet Potato Queenism. Play is magically restorative to your spirit—that's why I am exhorting everyone, everywhere, to come to Jackson, Mississippi, the third week-

273

end of each and every March to dress up funny and march down the street with me in the Million Queen March™ at Mal's St. Paddy's Parade—because I believe it will probably *save your life* to do so—and greatly enhance it at the same time. Go to the *"Gallery"* at www.sweetpotatoqueens.com and see if those folks don't look like they know something you need to know.

Your kids need to see you play—they need to see you having *fun* for no reason other than the sheer joy of having it. If they see you giving your time to playing, they get the message that "this is of value" and they will apply that to their own lives in the future.

It also helps them see you as a Person—with feelings and emotions and friends and a *life*—*not* just a Parent with none of those things. This may be a big surprise to your kids. "Parents" are, too often in kids' minds, nothing but buzz-killing, rule-making/enforcing, boring, life-is-work-all-the-time, everything-is-serious-business, *old* creatures who maybe *used to be* "people" a long time ago, but nobody in this house can remember when.

So, yeah, I think it's important for kids to see *us* acting silly and having fun—with stuff that doesn't necessarily *include them.* Gasp! Life that doesn't happen at their soccer/baseball/basketball/football games, dance recitals, and/or tennis tournaments? Life that doesn't even involve *children*? Is it still available?

We need to stay in practice doing this kind of thing—because, guess what?—they are *going* to grow up and *leave* in hardly any time a-tall, and we need to remember how to *dance* so that we are prepared to do it—in the driveway—as soon as their cars are out of sight.

We also need to play *with* them—and I'm not talking about organized games and sports, although there's room for that, too. But mostly I'm talking about just *playing*—at something that doesn't require a Rule Book and regulation gear and referees.

My daddy played so well that kids in our neighborhood would actually come over when they knew that my seester, Judy, and I were *gone,* and ask our mother if "her daddy could come out and play." He was a one-man barrel o' monkeys, he was.

He and Mama built us a swimming pool when I was in the first grade. When I say they built us a swimming pool, I mean the two of them *dug a hole* twelve feet wide, forty feet long, and four feet deep at one end and seven feet deep at the other—with *shovels* they dug this hole in the thick and heavy Mississippi clay of our backyard. Took 'em a while. Then they had some guys come and do the concrete work. It was not the best-looking thing you ever saw. The words "swimming *hole*" do come to mind, but Lord, how we loved it.

That Yazoo Clay soil of central Mississippi crawls and shifts constantly, so there were always many cracks and crevices in the walls and floor. Every spring, they would get out there and patch and paint the whole pool and then they filled it with the garden hose—which took several days of constant running, as you might imagine. But the day the hose was turned on was the most exciting day of the year.

All my childhood buddies would come running—Tommy and Davee and Timmy and Harry—and we would literally sit in the empty pool, watching the water level creep up. Once it was full, for the next four months, we got out only to eat and sleep. Thinking back on it now, I can't recall anybody getting out for any other reason—I guess we all must've just peed in the pool. Oh, well. We were always a close-knit bunch.

We were never allowed to swim without an adult actually sitting by the pool watching us, and so Mama, God love her—when did she ever get anything done in the summertime?—would sit out there every day for *hours,* watching us. Daddy lived out there with us on the weekends. The neighborhood-wide (our street and the street behind us) standing invitation that my parents issued to all the other parents was that any and all kids were welcome to swim anytime—whether we were home or not—as long as one of the parents came to watch them.

Although all the kids came to swim when *my* parents were watching, of course—not one single kid from my street ever came with a parent of their own to watch them. Not one—*not once.* And remember, this was back in the days before mothers worked outside the home. Out of my whole neighborhood, only *one* mother worked and none of the other dads traveled—only mine—and besides my folks, the parents of my favorite brothers, Tommy and Davee, from the street behind us, were the only parents who ever watched us swim. Pretty sad.

But I got a lifelong love for play from my parents—and I'm

grateful. After all, I have *the* best job in the world thanks to that love—as far as I know, I am the world's *only* full-time, professional Sweet Potato Queen. It also equipped me to play with my own little girl—and avoid hearing that endless refrain of "We're bo-o-ored" from summertime kids.

I'd load up Bailey and whatever buddies she wanted to bring along and off we'd go to my dear friend Dennis's condo complex, where, during the week, the pool was totally empty except for us and one old retired guy—a die-hard sun worshipper named "T.P." The first time I took them, I took along a book for myself, thinking the kids would play in the water and I'd read and bag rays (I'm also a die-hard sun worshipper, SPF 30 notwithstanding). Within about five minutes, the kids were driving me crazy—they were bo-o-ored. I sat up in disbelief— *bored*—in a *swimming pool*? That's not even possible.

Thirty seconds later, I had them laughing so hysterically they were in danger of drinking the pool dry, because not only had I demonstrated for them my stunning prowess at the art of Cannonball, nearly draining the pool with the resulting splash, but I had challenged them to produce anything equal to it. For the next two hours, it was nothing but run, leap, ball up, *splash*, swim to side, clamber out, and repeat.

About ten minutes into this contest, we couldn't help but notice that the old guy, T.P., had sat up—and was taking notice of our little competition. Presently, he started offering his unsolicited advice and opinion on our form and execution. I told him

I didn't think we'd be taking any verbal input from any mere *spectators*, but if he wanted to get up off his recliner and give us a little *demonstration*, well, then we'd see if we thought his opinion counted for anything.

It was just the break he'd been waiting for and he sprang up from that chair and commenced cannonballing like the kid he still was in his heart. I thought he was gonna cry when we had to leave that day, but we assured him we would be back the next day. "What time?" was all he wanted to know.

The next day, we returned at the promised time to find we had the pool to ourselves—no T.P. in sight. We thought perhaps he'd overdone it a bit the previous day and was inside recuperating. Proved we didn't know T.P. very well yet. A few minutes later, we heard a car pull into the parking lot rather speedily, and before the engine was turned off, we heard the opening and slamming of doors, followed by the scuffling of a good many feet.

We looked up and saw that we were being invaded by Old Guys. T.P. had rounded up his entire Old Guy Breakfast Club and brought them to the Cannonball Wars. There were swimsuited old guys running and hitting the water like so many wrinkled-up, baldheaded, belly-laughing bombs. Bailey and her buddies were agog, to say the least, for a moment or two, but they quickly embraced the newcomers and the competition heated up quickly.

We played with those old guys every day for the rest of the

summer and it would be hard to say who had more fun—me, the kids, or the old guys. I bought water pistols for everybody in case they lost interest in cannonballing. I also got my good friend Bill Brown to give me a whole big bunch of old tire inner tubes off all them big ole Pepsi trucks he's got running all over the state. I figured we prolly ought to add inner-tube races to the Condo Pool Olympic Games, and I was right—the old guys and the kids proved to be quite speedy on their tubes.

Then, of course, you have to push the tubes out from the wall and leap out, trying to land butt first in the center of the tube farthest away from the side. And then you *have* to see how many different ways you can "tump" over everybody else's inner tube. "Tump" is an apostrophe-free contraction of the words "turn over" and "dump," in case you didn't know.

So there was not a single still, quiet bloodthirsty-battle-free moment at Dennis's condo pool all summer long. And the Great Cannonball Championship of '99 is still talked about to this very day.

I won, of course—I *always* win at Cannonball Wars—I am undefeated in my lifetime and expect to go to my grave with an unsullied record—whether I die this afternoon or live to 112— *no one* will *ever* best me at cannonballing. But my baby girl will have a lifetime of laughs trying.

Endings

Good Night, Sweet Mamas, Wherever You Are

The good *Care and Feeding* author, Doc Holt, indicated a belief—and I absolutely concur albeit with a derisive snort—that the Nursing Mother should be as free as possible from unnecessary cares and worry—that her rest at night should be disturbed as little as possible. Excuse me—she has just given birth to a person who came with an accompanying set of very necessary cares, a multitude of ceaseless worries, and an inexhaustible supply of different ways to shatter sleep. This woman will never be care- nor worry-free again as long as she lives, and she will only *truly* sleep again when she's dead.

I will never forget the moment at which the enormity of what I had done slammed into me like a semi hauling hogs. It was the day we were taking Peep home from the hospital. Waiting for the nurse to bring the mandatory wheelchair for my ride downstairs to the car, I was sitting in the rocker in my hospital room and Peep was lying in my lap, her head on my knees, her little feet against my tummy. I was gazing besottedly at her beautiful little face and generally feeling like this whole Mom Thing was exceptionally swell, when, with no warning whatsoever, Peep pushed her feet hard against me and straightened out her little legs—which had the horrifying effect of nearly launching her off my lap headfirst onto the cold, hard linoleum floor.

It didn't happen. With an instinct and speed—both new and unfamiliar to me—my hands caught her, but the awful knowledge of "what could have happened" was born in my heart in that instant and I was filled with absolute terror at the very thought of loving anybody *this much*. I grasped the full measure of the human heart's capacity for boundless love and transcendent joy—and I got the merest glimmer of its potential for being truly and utterly broken. At that moment, I knew that I could bear, believe, hope, and endure all things—for the sake of this little bitty baby girl on my lap. And so, we began our hopeful, happy, and, yes, sometimes harrowing journey together as Mother and Daughter. Worth it? Oh, yeah.

Okay, I wrote that stuff last month. Today is May 14, 2007, it is noon the day after Mother's Day, and so far, it has been the Worst and Best Day of My Life. My daughter, Bailey—who did *not* fall off my lap when she was five days old—is an absolutely beautiful nineteen-year-old. She just completed her freshman year at the University of Mississippi — we think she may even have straight As this semester. Her stepdad, Kyle, and I have just made an offer on a condo for her in Oxford, Mississippi, so she can live off campus for the next six years while she gets her law degree. I went to bed last night — and I got up this morning — thinking things really could not be more perfect in our lives at this moment.

Then the phone rang.

It was Bailey's dad — MoonPie — asking me if I had spoken to Bailey yet this morning, and I said no, and no surprise there, since it was around eight a.m., which, even in Mississippi, is considerably before noon. I don't generally expect to hear much from my daughter before midday unless she's working or going to school because if there is not a compelling force rousting her out of bed early, she will remain there for a large part of the day, arising at her leisure.

MoonPie said that although she had told him she would be spending the night at his house last night, she was not there and had not been there, she was not answering her phone, *and* he'd just heard that there had been a one-car wreck involving an SUV, two teenagers, and a fatality — in his neighborhood in the wee hours of the morning.

I find it hard to write any more about this — and by that, I mean I find it hard to form a thought in my head and get it to go from there to my fingers on the keyboard. If you are a parent, you can imagine this feeling. I couldn't tell you a single thought that came to me in those moments. One second, I was enjoying the early morning song of the mockingbirds, and the next second, the phone was ringing and someone was telling me that my only child might well be lying horribly injured, alone, and unidentified in an unknown hospital—which, when I allowed my brain to go anywhere *near* that other possibility, seemed, by comparison, like it might be my deepest wish.

My initial reaction was involuntary—I felt myself fold up and sink to my knees, trying to find something in my mind to focus on—some action to take—some words to say besides, *"God, NO!"* and its alternate, *"Please God!"*

My neighbor Angie heard me and came running. While I put in calls to everybody I could think of who might know where she could be—plus every emergency room in town—and finally, dear God in Heaven, the coroner's office, Angie called my husband, Kyle, The Cutest Boy in the World and also *THE* Most Crisis-Capable Man in the Universe. (I had sent him to Arkansas to visit his precious mama—and daddy—for Mother's Day while I stayed behind to write this book.)

The hospitals were able to tell me immediately that they did not have her. The coroner's office said they would have to check to be certain and call me back. Thankfully, within minutes—the longest ones of my entire life—and before I heard anything from the coroner, Kyle, from the side of a mountain in Arkansas, had managed to do what none of us here were able to do—he found my baby girl, very much alive and totally safe. So, twice in the space of an hour, one sentence spoken on a telephone sent me to my knees—but this time in hysterical disbelief and heart-nearly-broken-in-two gratitude for the message received.

In a bizarre coincidence, Key, the precious young man who lost his life, and Jessica, the darling girl so frightfully injured in that horrible accident, were dear friends of Bailey's—but after my own terror, it would have been no different even if they'd been strangers to us—I felt a bond—a kinship of unthinkable pain and loss with those other mothers—the one sitting by that hospital bed, gratefully watching her little girl breathe in and out and thinking that, all things considered, her lucky stars are innumerable—and the other, utterly brokenhearted one for whom that most dreadful bell tolled that morning.

Oh, mercy, Lord, it's been a tough May. Only a few days after that tragedy, I got word that Freda Holmes—Mama Freda—my second mama by choice—was dying. It hasn't been that long since I delivered the eulogy at the funeral of her daughter, Cindy, one of my lifelong best friends. I couldn't believe I was going to lose Freda now as well.

Shortly before Mother's Day, I had gone to see Freda, knowing that she'd had some tests run. I took her the first copy of this book's cover, which I'd just gotten that day, along with the book's dedication that I had written to her. Cindy's daughter Deenie, who has the sweet heart of her late and so much-lamented mama, was there, having flown home from Los Angeles to go with Freda, or "Ta," as they called her ("dear one" in her native Lebanese), to receive the doctor's diagnosis. Cindy's other daughter, Neecie, was there, along with Cindy's brothers, John and George—and we all had such a good visit—many laughs and, as always, a few tears for our Cindy. I brought a copy of the first chapter—jokingly telling Freda that Deenie could read it to her—since Deenie's the only one in the family who is known to share my propensity for "all those words"—the ones with four letters.

The very next week, Deenie called to tell me the diagnosis and the prognosis: It was cancer of the most catastrophic order and the time was short. Deenie urged me to come soon if I wanted to say good-bye. I went the moment we hung up the phone.

It was shocking to see such a rapid decline in this woman who'd always been such a powerful force for good in my life. The disease was rampant and ravaging her body, she was on massive amounts of painkillers and could barely speak, but Deenie and I were able to make her laugh several times. Then, alone with my Mama Freda for a few minutes, I held her hands and looked deep into those gorgeous Lebanese brown eyes and told her, one last time, how very much I loved her and how grateful I will always be to her for her love and for the life-changing lessons I had learned from her. With my very soul, I thanked her—one last time. She smiled at me and said, "So precious, you are so precious, darlin'." Those are the last words she ever spoke to me and I will carry them with me always. I feel precious because she deemed me so.

Freda knew what she meant to me because I had written her a long letter about it some years back. It meant as much to her to hear from me how much I felt she had changed my life as her loving actions had meant toward me. I have always been glad I told her.

I'm sure, if you think about it for even a moment, there is a Freda in your life somewhere. A woman or a man—not your own mother or father—from whom you have received a great blessing. And this is not to say that your parents were bad or unloving or that they failed you in any way. Perhaps it's just that this one special thing was something that, for whatever reason, you didn't—or would not allow yourself to—get from your own family, but you got it from your special person, your "Freda." Your life is somehow different—and immeasurably better—because of the gift that person gave you.

God does pay attention. There is absolutely no lack of love in this world—because there is no lack of *people* in this world, and, as people, we are God's Eyes to see the needs of others, God's Hands to care for one another, God's Heart to show love where it's needed. Sometimes, it doesn't come from the places we expect and it doesn't always look the way we expect it to look—but what we need *is* there, if we're willing to recognize and receive it.

I hope that you'll take the time to acknowledge the Freda in your life, and then, I really hope you'll look for the child in your life who really needs a Freda in theirs. Teach a kid to throw a ball and tell her she's really good at it. Pass on your favorite biscuit recipe to a youngster and tell him he's a natural in the kitchen. Tell 'em all they're smart and funny and good-looking. And precious—tell 'em all how very precious they are. Everybody needs to make it their Life's Work to teach at least *one* kid to say, *"WHEE!"* and mean it.

Acknowledgments

I cannot believe I finally got permission to use the photo that graces the cover of this book. It is probably my All-Time Favorite Photograph in the History of the Entire World Living or Dead—and the subject is, of course, my All-Time Favorite PERSON in the History of the Entire World Living or Dead. So thanks, *bébé*. And thanks to Marion and Gary Silber for capturing that priceless smile for all time.

My extremely cute and talented agent, Jenny Bent of Trident Media Group, continues to use her cuteness and her talent in her tireless efforts on my behalf, and I remain forever grateful to her for this. Even though she did NOT name Isobel after me, I am still grateful to her for all the things she does do.

The Dream Team at Simon & Schuster: Denise Roy, Julia Prosser, Kate Ankofski, David Rosenthal, Deb Darrock,

Aileen Boyle, Victoria Meyer, Deirdre Mueller, Leah Wasielewski, Jackie Seow, Sybil Pincus, and Dana Sloan. A million, billion thanks for the million, billion things you do—and do—and do—for little ole me.

Alycia Jones and Sarajean Babin—if y'all ever leave me, I'm quitting—just so you know.

Liza and Rick Looser and the incredibly gifted crew at the Cirlot Agency continue to make www.sweetpotatoqueens.com the best Web site anywhere. God bless you every one.

Frank Drennan and Capitol City Beverages were early supporters of the Sweet Potato Queens. As a matter of fact, Frank (or Dink, as we call him) paid for our very first outfits AND he used to let us build the float in his beer warehouses. We're hoping he's a sponsor for the Million Queen March in '08, but even if he's not, he's been a Spud Stud from the git-go and we will always love him for it.

I am still in love with The Cutest Boy in the World, and I'm so lucky that somewhere there's a bona fide legal document that declares me to be Mrs. Kyle Jennings.

Bad Dog Management is still guarding the Queendom, and I am grateful for the 24/7 protection.

And in case I didn't work in enough stories about my nearest and dearest—they don't like it if they're not in my books—HERE ARE Y'ALL'S NAMES, in NO particular order: Jim Sumner, Joanie Bailey—also Buster Bailey, who just looooves to find himself in my pages, George Ewing, Smokey Davis,

Ellyn Weeks, Allison Church, Katie Dezember Werdel (you'll always be Katie Christmas to us!) and her shiny new hubby Tim, Elizabeth Jackson, Melanie Jeffreys, Cynthia Speetjens, Jeffrey Gross, Allen Payne, Judy Palmer, Randy Wallace, Angie Gray, Wilson Wong, Laura Lynn, John Cartwright, Melissa Manchester, Sharon Vaughn, Rupert Holmes, Kevin DeRemer, Larry Bouchea, Joe Speetjens, Mike Babin, Russell Jones, Steven Jeffreys, and Carl Kolb. Thank you all for Meritorious Service in the Name of Love.